Python Uncoiled: From Statements to Power Scripts

Introduction:

If you've picked up this book, congratulations—you've already taken the first step toward becoming a certified snake charmer. Not the kind with baskets and flutes, but the kind who can bend computers to their will using nothing more than well-placed indentation and a few magical keywords. This is Python, baby—where readability reigns, whitespace isn't just cosmetic, and the code practically reads like bedtime poetry (with fewer dragons and more dictionaries).

Maybe you've heard the buzz. "Python is great for beginners!" they said. "It's perfect for data science!" others claimed. "Even kids are learning it!" shouted someone from a tech meetup while dual-wielding espresso shots. And while all of that is true, Python is more than just friendly—it's sneakily powerful. Like a rubber duck that transforms into a laser cannon when nobody's looking. This book is your official guide to that transformation.

We're going to start small—**very** small. Your first taste of code will be a humble `print()` statement, possibly greeting the world, or maybe just whispering existential doubts into the terminal. But don't be fooled. That single line of code? It's a gateway drug. Before you know it, you'll be storing data in variables, building functions, looping through logic like a caffeinated squirrel, and even writing scripts that do things *while you nap*. Yes, automation is legal here—and wildly addictive.

What makes Python special is that it doesn't punish you for not knowing everything. It's the language equivalent of a patient teacher who lets you ask "But why?" five times in a row without flipping a desk. You don't need to memorize 1,000 commands or wrestle with convoluted syntax to do cool things. Python is clean, clear, and charmingly intuitive. It's the IKEA furniture of programming—only, you won't be left with five extra screws and emotional damage afterward.

This book doesn't aim to impress you with ten-dollar words or academic posturing. We're not here to make you feel under qualified or unworthy of writing code. Instead, we're going to build your skills one delightful, digestible bite at a time—with examples, metaphors, and maybe a few code-based dad jokes to keep things spicy. (If you're the type to chuckle at `Why do Python devs prefer snakes over dogs? Because they don't need paws for thought`, then you're in the right place.)

By the time you finish, you'll be armed with real-world Python skills. We'll delve into data types, conditionals, loops, lists, file handling, error management, modules, and even dabble in more advanced arenas like APIs, web scraping, and automation. You'll gain the confidence to write scripts that save you hours of work—or make your friends think you're some sort of low-key cyber wizard.

And don't worry, we'll celebrate your bugs too. Because coding isn't about writing flawless programs from day one—it's about learning, experimenting, and occasionally muttering "why won't you run" before realizing you misspelled "print" as "pront." Python's error messages are surprisingly helpful, and this book will help you interpret them like ancient scrolls revealing the secrets of logic and syntax.

So whether you're brand new to programming or switching from another language that gave you trust issues (looking at you, C++), consider this your comfy on-ramp to something awesome. Python is approachable, adaptable, and incredibly relevant in today's tech landscape. And together, we're going to uncoil this majestic language—from the first print statement to power scripts that hum like finely tuned engines.

Let's plug in, fire up that terminal, and get started. Because the only thing better than writing Python… is writing it with confidence, clarity, and just a little bit of swagger.

Table of Contents

Chapter 1: Hello, World! – Your First Python Handshake

- Setting up Python without summoning demons

- Writing your first `print()` like a proud parent

- Understanding the beauty of whitespace and indentation

Chapter 2: Variables – Taming Tiny Data Beasts

- Naming things without causing an identity crisis

- Understanding types: integers, floats, strings, oh my

- Swapping, reassigning, and juggling values like a pro

Chapter 3: Strings Attached – Playing with Text

- Concatenation, repetition, and string formatting magic

- Escaping characters (and maybe your coding anxiety)

- F-strings: Because old-school formatting is so 2015

Chapter 4: Numbers Don't Lie – But They Might Divide Funny

- Basic math in Python: Addition to exponentiation

- Integer division vs. float division (a spicy debate)

- The modulus operator and other hidden treasures

Chapter 5: Booleans & Conditionals – Making Decisions Without Regret

- Truthiness, falsiness, and logical operators

- `if`, `elif`, and `else` – the holy trinity of choices

- Writing cleaner, smarter conditional code

Chapter 6: Loops – Repeating Yourself Elegantly

- `while` and `for` loops – your code's personal workout plan

- Looping through ranges, lists, and strings

- `break` and `continue` – your flow control ninjas

Chapter 7: Lists – The Grocery Bag of Python

- Creating, modifying, and slicing lists like sushi

- List methods: append, pop, sort, and more

- Nested lists and list comprehensions (sneaky but cool)

Chapter 8: Dictionaries – Keys, Values, and Chaos Organized

- Creating dictionaries: curly braces and cleverness

- Accessing, adding, and updating values

- Looping through dicts without losing your mind

Chapter 9: Tuples & Sets – The Low-Maintenance Siblings

- Tuples: immutable and proud

- Sets: the rebel data type with no duplicates

- Sending HTTP requests with `requests`

- Parsing JSON responses and doing cool things with them

Chapter 16: Regular Expressions – Text Searching with a Secret Code

- The weird and wonderful world of regex

- Matching, searching, and substituting patterns

- Avoiding common regex rage moments

Chapter 17: Web Scraping – Python, the Data Thief (for Good)

- Introduction to `BeautifulSoup` and `requests`

- Extracting data from real websites (legally, please)

- Cleaning and storing scraped data like a champ

Chapter 18: Automation – Make Your Computer Do the Boring Stuff

- Automating tasks with scripts and schedules

- Sending emails, renaming files, and clicking buttons

- Using `pyautogui` and `schedule` for everyday sorcery

Chapter 19: Virtual Environments – Keeping Your Dependencies in Line

- What is a virtual environment and why should you care?

- Creating, activating, and deactivating environments

- Managing multiple projects like a Python professional

Chapter 20: Testing & Debugging – Because Bugs Are Eternal

- Writing unit tests using `unittest` and `pytest`

- Using breakpoints and the `pdb` debugger

- Test-driven development (or pretending you planned it all along)

Chapter 21: Data Handling – CSVs, Excel, and Pandas, Oh My!

Chapter 22: Power Scripts – Python in the Real World

Chapter 1: Hello, World! – Your First Python Handshake

1.
Welcome, code crusader, to the very first step on your Python-powered journey. Before you panic, no, you don't need to know what "object-oriented" means yet. In fact, if your only programming experience is yelling at your printer, you're in the right place. This chapter is your first taste of Python—no prerequisites, no pressure. You'll write a single line of code and make your computer talk to you like it finally respects you. It's a rite of passage for coders worldwide. And it starts with something deceptively simple: `print("Hello, world!")`. But behind that innocent message lies your entry ticket to building games, apps, automation, and even AI overlords.

2.
Let's talk about what you'll need first. Python doesn't require a wizard's robe, but it *does* require installation. Head over to python.org and download the latest version—don't worry, it's free, and so far, no one's gotten cursed. If you're on Windows, check the box that says "Add Python to PATH," or future-you will not be pleased. On macOS, Python 3 may already be lurking in your terminal—like a quiet ninja waiting to be summoned. Linux users, you're already in the cool kids' club; just make sure you have Python 3 and not its ancient cousin, Python 2. Once installed, open your terminal or command prompt and type `python --version`. If it replies with a version starting with "3," congratulations—you've summoned the snake.

3.
Now, let's actually write some Python. You can launch the Python interpreter (also known as the

REPL: Read-Eval-Print Loop) by typing `python` or `python3` in your terminal. You'll be greeted by a few lines of friendly text, followed by those famous three greater-than signs (`>>>`) —this is your Python playground. Type this in exactly: `print("Hello, world!")` and press Enter. Behold! Your machine speaks! It outputs: `Hello, world!`, and just like that, you've written your first working program. No compiling. No rituals. Just elegant simplicity.

4.

Let's unpack that little miracle of code. The `print()` function is Python's way of saying, "Here, let me show you something." It takes whatever you put inside the parentheses and spits it out for the world (or just your terminal) to see. The double quotes indicate that you're working with a string—a series of characters treated as text. You could just as easily say `print("I'm learning Python!")`, or even `print("Please send coffee.")`. The key is the syntax: function name, parentheses, and quotation marks. Forget semicolons; Python doesn't need that noise. This is clean code for civilized people.

5.

Now, some people ask, "Why 'Hello, world!'?" Is it tradition? Is it superstition? Maybe it's just the programmer's equivalent of a handshake or a digital first date. The phrase dates back to the 1970s, first seen in a C programming manual. Since then, it's become the universal icebreaker between humans and machines. It's short, sweet, and universally recognizable. Think of it as the secret password to the world of coding.

6.

If you're the curious type (and we hope you are), try changing what's inside the quotation marks. Go ahead and type `print("Python is awesome!")`. Boom! You've now customized your output. Try using single quotes instead of double quotes: `print('Python rocks!')`—it still works. Python is flexible that way, as long as you're consistent. Just don't mix and match quotes on the same line unless you enjoy syntax errors. Think of Python like a grammar nerd—it's chill until you mess with its punctuation.

7.

So what happens if you forget the closing quote? Or the parenthesis? Let's find out. Try this: `print("Oops!` and hit Enter. Python will shout at you—not rudely, but firmly—with a `SyntaxError`. This is its way of saying, "Hey, something's not right." Mistakes are not just allowed, they're encouraged. Every error is a clue, not a catastrophe. Get comfy with seeing red text—it's how we learn.

8.

Speaking of errors, let's explore how Python communicates them. When you break a rule, Python throws an error message, complete with a line number and a clue. For instance, `SyntaxError: EOL while scanning string literal` is Python's poetic way of saying, "You forgot to close your string, friend." These messages might look cryptic at first, but they're golden breadcrumbs. Reading them is like listening to your code talk back. Debugging is basically having a conversation with your confused computer. Listen closely, and it'll tell you where it hurts.

9.

Let's spice things up—try printing multiple messages. You can write `print("First line")` and then another line like `print("Second line")`. Run those back to back, and you've got a mini-script! But what if you want to print both on the same line? You can combine them like this: `print("First line", "Second line")`. Python will separate them with a space by default. You can even tell Python how to separate them using the `sep` argument. Try this: `print("First", "Second", sep="-")` and smile at your hyphenated handiwork.

10.

Alright, let's talk about comments—those sneaky lines that don't get run but explain what's going on. In Python, comments start with the pound sign (#). Try this: `# This is a comment` and nothing happens. That's the point. Comments are for humans, not the interpreter. They help you remember why your future code looks like it was written by a sleep-deprived squirrel. Write comments. Your future self will thank you.

11.

Now that you've printed a few lines and scared off a few syntax errors, you might be wondering: where do I write real programs? Good question. So far, we've been using the REPL, which is great for quick tests. But for longer code, you'll want to use a script file. Create a new file named `hello.py` and open it in a text editor or IDE like VS Code. Inside it, write `print("Hello again, world!")`. Save the file, then run it from your terminal with `python hello.py`.

12.

Running a Python script feels a bit like launching a rocket—even if all it does is print a message. You just entered the world of *scripting*. That `.py` file is your code capsule, ready to be deployed anywhere Python lives. You can email it, share it, even sneak it into a Raspberry Pi and feel like a hacker. Scripts can hold hundreds or thousands of lines of logic. But for now, one line is just fine. Every great script starts small.

13.

Let's experiment with some fun output. Try printing art! Type this:

```python
CopyEdit
print("  /\\_/\\\n ( o.o )\n  > ^ <")
```

You just created a cat using escape characters. The `\n` tells Python to move to a new line. Escape characters are like stage directions for your text. They help you format, tab, or even insert quotes into quotes. Yes, Python is secretly a theater nerd.

14.

Escape characters are a great way to spice up your output. For example, `\t` adds a tab, while `\\` lets you print an actual backslash. Want quotes inside quotes? Use opposite types: `print('He` said `"hi"'`). Or escape them: `print("He said \"hi\"")`. Don't worry—you'll get used to typing slashes like it's second nature. It's all part of Python's charm. And it lets you write expressive, formatted text like a code poet.

15.

Let's play with math—Python loves math more than most middle schoolers. Try `print(3 + 4)` and watch it do the arithmetic. You can also subtract, multiply with `*`, and divide with `/`. Want powers? Use `**`, like `print(2 ** 3)` to get 8. Python evaluates these in a predictable order (remember PEMDAS?). It's basically a calculator that never runs out of batteries. And it's one you can *program* to do whatever you want.

16.

You can even combine text and math, but carefully. If you try `print("Result: " + 5)`, Python will throw a tantrum. That's because it won't automatically convert numbers into strings —you have to do it yourself with `str()`. So, write `print("Result: " + str(5))` and it'll purr with approval. This is your first encounter with **type casting**—the gentle art of changing one type into another. It's not scary. It's just like translating between languages: Python to human, and vice versa.

17.

Let's take a quick peek under the hood. Every value in Python—strings, numbers, functions— has a type. You can check it by using `type()`. Try `print(type("hello"))` and `print(type(42))`. Python will proudly announce: `<class 'str'>` and `<class 'int'>`. This tells you exactly what you're dealing with, which is handy for debugging. Knowing the type of a thing is like knowing whether you're holding a cat or a chainsaw— important context.

18.

Feeling bold? Try assigning your output to a variable. Type `greeting = "Hello, world!"`, then `print(greeting)`. Bam—Python remembers your message. Variables are like labeled jars for your data: you fill them once, then reuse them however you like. Don't worry, we'll go deep into variables next chapter. For now, pat yourself on the back—you're already thinking like a programmer. You're storing data and calling it by name. That's power.

19.

Let's recap what you've done so far: installed Python, launched the interpreter, wrote your first line of code, and caused your computer to respond politely. You learned how to print messages, handle errors, escape characters, and store strings in variables. That's not just progress—it's a mini-miracle. This is how every developer started—one `print()` at a time. And you've already built your first foundation. Keep building. The view from higher up gets even better.

20.

Before we wrap, here's your first challenge: write a short Python script that prints your name, a fun fact, and your favorite number. Bonus points if you format it like a mini bio! You'll practice `print()`, string formatting, and maybe even some math. Save it as `my_intro.py` and run it from your terminal. Show it off to a friend, your cat, or your inner imposter syndrome. You've earned it. Python doesn't judge.

21.

Remember, Python doesn't care if you're 9 or 99. It doesn't care if you've never coded a day in your life. It just wants you to *try*. And with each try, you'll get better, bolder, and more confident. Mistakes are part of the magic—don't be afraid to break things. That's how builders learn. And by picking up this book, you've already proven you're ready to build.

22.

In the next chapter, we'll dive into variables—how to create them, name them, and convince them to do your bidding. We'll turn Python into your digital filing cabinet, storing data and ideas with tidy efficiency. But for now, bask in your success. You made Python talk. You've shaken hands with the snake—and it didn't bite. Instead, it smiled and said:

```python
CopyEdit
print("Welcome to Python!")
```

Chapter 2: Variables – Taming Tiny Data Beasts

1.

Now that you've said hello to the world like a polite digital citizen, it's time to teach your code how to *remember things*. Enter variables—Python's equivalent of labeled jars, lockers, or enchanted scrolls that store your precious data. Variables allow your code to hold on to information and use it later, like a squirrel hoarding acorns for a cold day of automation. Think of them as named containers that can hold almost anything: numbers, text, booleans, even other variables. Want to store your name? Easy. Want to store the meaning of life? Sure—`answer = 42` and you're now a philosopher-programmer. Variables are the very foundation of programs that think, respond, calculate, and adapt. Without them, your code would have the memory span of a goldfish.

2.

In Python, creating a variable is blissfully simple. You don't need to declare types, call the variable fairy, or write an essay—just assign a value with =. For example: `name = "Ada"` creates a variable called `name` and stores the string `"Ada"` inside it. Want to change the value? Just reassign it: `name = "Grace"`. Python won't nag you about changing types either—`name = 42` is perfectly valid. This flexibility is part of what makes Python so beginner-friendly (and occasionally so chaotic). You don't have to worry about strict types—Python figures it out for you, like a very supportive but chill friend. Just remember: the variable goes on the left, and the value goes on the right.

3.

Let's meet the primitive data types: `int`, `float`, `str`, and `bool`. `int` is for whole numbers like 7, 42, or 1984—no decimal drama. `float` handles decimal numbers like 3.14 or -0.001—great for things like pizza slices and scientific calculations. `str` is short for string, which holds text wrapped in quotes—double or single, Python's not picky. `bool` represents truth values: `True` or `False` (capitalized because Python is fancy like that). Assigning these types to variables is seamless: `age = 30`, `pi = 3.14`, `quote = "Code is poetry"`, `is_human = True`. Each one brings its own superpowers to your coding arsenal. And don't worry—we'll unpack them all in due time.

4.

Naming your variables is both an art and a science. Python has a few rules: names must start with a letter or underscore, can contain numbers, but can't start with a number. Avoid spaces, special characters, or naming your variable `print` unless you enjoy chaos. Use lowercase letters and underscores for readability, like `first_name` or `total_price`. Descriptive names beat cryptic ones every time—`temperature_celsius` is better than `x`. That said, don't go overboard with names like
`this_variable_holds_the_result_of_the_operation_that_averag es_temperatures`. Keep it simple, memorable, and non-repetitive. In short: clarity beats cleverness.

5.

Let's try it in action. Open your Python interpreter or script file and type: `pet_name = "Bubbles"`. Then, type `print(pet_name)`. Boom—your variable speaks! You can even assign it to a new variable: `favorite_pet = pet_name`. Try `print(favorite_pet)` and watch as Python carries your data like a loyal assistant. Variables are all about references—they *point* to values stored in memory. You don't need to know how the memory works just yet. Just know that Python remembers for you.

6.

Let's dive into numbers. Try this: `apples = 5`, then `oranges = 3`. Now do some arithmetic: `total = apples + oranges`. Print `total`, and Python will give you 8. You just stored numbers, added them, and saved the result. You could even subtract: `difference = apples - oranges`, or multiply: `basket = apples * oranges`. Want division? `ratio = apples / oranges` works too—and returns a float. Python handles math like a caffeinated calculator.

7.

Mixing variables and strings opens the door to dynamic output. Let's say you have `name = "Ada"` and `age = 30`. Try this: `print("Name:", name, "Age:", age)` and admire the magic. You can even format it more elegantly with an f-string: `print(f"{name} is {age} years old")`. F-strings let you embed variables directly into strings—no awkward plus signs or type casting. It's like Python saying, "Don't worry, I got this." Just use `f"Text {variable}"` and Python will do the interpolation. It's clean, readable, and oddly satisfying.

8.

You can change variable values at any time—Python doesn't get clingy. If you start with `score = 10` and later write `score = 20`, Python updates it instantly. Variables are mutable in that sense—they point to a value, not chain you to one. You can even swap values:

```python
CopyEdit
a = 5
b = 10
a, b = b, a
```
Now `a` is 10 and `b` is 5. Python swaps like a magician flipping cards.

9.

Let's talk about `None`. This special value represents the absence of value—it's Python's version of "I got nothin'." Assign it with `user_input = None` when you don't have a value *yet*. It's commonly used as a placeholder or sentinel value. You can later check for it with: `if user_input is None:`. It helps your code say, "Hey, something's missing here, and that's okay (for now)." Just don't try to add it to numbers or strings—it's not that kind of party. `None` is the elegant way to say "not applicable."

10.

You can also perform multiple assignments in one line. Try this: `x, y, z = 1, 2, 3`. Each variable gets assigned in order—no loops or extra effort. You can even assign the same value to multiple variables: `a = b = c = 0`. Python doesn't mind. But be careful—changing `a` won't magically update `b` and `c`. They all reference the same value *initially*, but they're still separate names. It's efficient, but best used with simple types like numbers.

11.

Need to delete a variable? Use `del variable_name`. For example, `del x` removes `x` from memory. Try printing it after that, and Python will bark: `NameError: name 'x' is not defined`. This is how you Marie Kondo your variables. Only keep what sparks joy —or at least, doesn't break your script. Usually, Python handles cleanup automatically. But sometimes, you just want a clean slate. `del` is your digital broom.

12.

Python has some reserved words you can't use as variable names. These include classics like `if`, `else`, `for`, `while`, `class`, `def`, and more. Try naming a variable `def` and Python will look at you like you just insulted its ancestry. These keywords have specific jobs in the language. Think of them like seats already taken at the dinner table. You're welcome to dine, but don't try to steal the chef's apron. You can always check the full list by importing the `keyword` module and calling `keyword.kwlist`.

13.

Variables can hold more than just simple values. They can hold lists, dictionaries, tuples—even functions. Try this wild one:

```python
CopyEdit
def greet():
    return "Hello!"
say_hi = greet
print(say_hi())
```

You just assigned a function to a variable and called it like a boss. Python is flexible like that. Your variables can hold a universe of functionality.

14.

Let's peek at some best practices for variable naming. Use lowercase with underscores for multi-word names (`user_name`, not `username` or `UserName`). Avoid single-letter variables unless you're doing math or trying to be cryptic. Keep it descriptive—`tax_rate` is way better than `x1`. Don't be afraid to be verbose if it helps clarity. Future-you (and collaborators) will thank you. The best variable names feel like natural language. They reduce bugs and improve readability like little code vitamins.

15.

Case matters in Python. `Speed`, `speed`, and `SPEED` are all different variables. Python is case-sensitive, unlike your friendly email app. This means you have to be precise, or you'll confuse the poor interpreter. So be consistent with your casing. Pick a style and stick to it. There's no "close enough" in Python—only correct or crash. Precision is your new best friend.

16.

Let's say you want to see what's inside your variable. You already know `print()` will do the trick, but for debugging, you can combine it with `type()` or `id()`. `type()` shows what kind of thing you're working with. `id()` shows its memory address—a unique number Python uses to track objects. This is useful when comparing variable references. Not all equals are created equal. Understanding what your variable *is* helps you write smarter code.

17.

Variables can be used to create more variables. Like, `a = 5`, then `b = a + 10`. Python does the math and assigns `b` the value 15. This is how you start building logic. It's not just storing values—it's performing operations, making decisions, adapting to input. Variables are the lifeblood of dynamic code. Without them, every program would be a static painting. With them, your code becomes an interactive story.

18.

Sometimes you'll want user input—something that changes each time the code runs. You can ask for it with `input()`:

```python
CopyEdit
name = input("What's your name? ")
print(f"Hello, {name}!")
```

Whatever the user types gets stored in the variable. Just remember: `input()` always returns a string. If you need a number, convert it with `int()` or `float()`. User input makes your program feel alive—and a little unpredictable.

19.

It's time for a mini recap. You've learned how to create variables, name them, assign values, swap them, and even ask the user for input. That's a huge step forward! You now understand how Python remembers data and reuses it. This is how we build logic, store state, and make code smarter. These "tiny data beasts" you've tamed? They're the muscle behind every meaningful app, game, and automation script. The fun is just beginning. And soon, we'll be working with **lists**—like variables with built-in backpacks.

20.

Here's a mini challenge: write a script that stores your name, age, and favorite food. Print them out using an f-string. Then reassign each variable with new values and print again. Try combining them into a sentence like, "My name is Scott, I'm 35, and I love sushi." You'll be flexing your variable muscles and building your coding reflexes. Try mixing strings with numbers and use `str()` where needed. Be bold—Python's got your back. And so do I.

21.

As we continue our journey, remember that variables are your building blocks. Everything complex in Python is made from simple things like numbers, strings, and booleans—all stored in variables. Mastering them early makes every future lesson easier. Don't just use variables— *understand* them. They're more than containers—they're your bridge between thinking and doing. Python gives you power by letting you name, store, and reuse *anything*. That's not just programming—that's digital alchemy. And you, my friend, are the alchemist.

22.

Next up, we're diving into **strings**—those lovable little sequences of characters that make your programs sing. We'll cover how to build them, break them, slice them, and dance with them using Python's powerful tools. You'll learn how to manipulate text like a command-line Shakespeare. For now, take a breath, enjoy what you've learned, and maybe assign a compliment to a variable: `compliment = "You're doing great!"`. Then print it. Because you are doing great. Onward to Chapter 3, where Python gets poetic.

Chapter 3: Strings Attached – Playing with Text

1.

If variables are your data storage, then **strings** are your favorite kind of luggage—perfect for carrying text, quotes, jokes, and questionable emoji poetry. A **string** is just a sequence of characters wrapped in either single or double quotes. That's right: `"Hello"` and `'Hello'` are both strings, and Python doesn't play favorites. Strings are everywhere—usernames, email addresses, tweets, even sarcastic error messages. And lucky for us, Python gives strings a royal treatment. You can store them, manipulate them, compare them, and even slice them like digital sushi. Strings are fun, flexible, and slightly dramatic—just like theater kids with built-in formatting. Ready to make your code sing? Let's pull those strings.

2.

Creating a string is as easy as declaring your undying love for pizza. Just wrap your message in quotes: `message = "I love Python"`. Want to use single quotes instead? `message = 'Python is love'` works just as well. What if your string *needs* quotes inside it? Use alternating styles: `'He said "Python is cool"'` or `"Don't stop coding!"`. If you want quotes within quotes *within* quotes, Python will politely ask you to calm down. For more complex strings, you can escape quotes with a backslash: `"She said, \"Hello there!\""` keeps everything civilized. Don't worry—it's less chaotic than it sounds.

3.

Let's print a string and admire the simplicity.

```python
CopyEdit
greeting = "Hello, world!"
print(greeting)
```

Python happily outputs the message—no fanfare, just clarity. Want to add flair? Use string concatenation:

```python
CopyEdit
first = "Python"
second = "Rocks"
print(first + " " + second)
```

Boom—custom messages stitched together with style. Strings aren't just data; they're building blocks for personality in code.

4.

But hold your plus signs—concatenation can get clunky. Enter **f-strings**, Python's gift to readability. They let you insert variables into strings like a boss:

```python
CopyEdit
name = "Tina"
print(f"Hi, {name}!")
```

F-strings start with `f` before the quotes and use curly braces for variables. You can even include expressions:

```python
CopyEdit
print(f"{name} has {len(name)} letters.")
```

It's string interpolation, minus the drama and backslashes.

5.

Strings are basically arrays of characters, and that means—you guessed it—**indexing**. The first character is at position 0, so `name[0]` gives you `'T'`. `name[1]` gives `'i'`, and so on. Negative indexing? Oh yes. `name[-1]` gives the last character, which is `'a'` here. Strings are your digital scrolls, and indexing is your magnifying glass. Just remember: out-of-range indexes will cause Python to freak out with an `IndexError`. Respect the bounds, and you'll be fine.

6.

Want to slice a string? Go full Fruit Ninja with the slicing syntax: `string[start:end]`. For example: `word = "Python"`, `print(word[0:3])` gives `'Pyt'`. Notice it includes the **start index** but excludes the **end index**—Python's version of open-ended relationships. You can omit the start to begin at 0, or omit the end to go all the way. `word[:4]` gives `'Pyth'`, and `word[2:]` gives `'thon'`. Slicing is extremely handy for parsing input, trimming output, and generally looking smart at parties. Use it wisely.

7.

Let's talk about **len()**, the measuring tape for strings. Try `len("Banana")` and you'll get 6. Spaces and punctuation count too—Python isn't picky. This is your go-to for size checking, formatting, and bragging about long names. Use it in conditionals, loops, and anywhere you need to know how "thicc" your string is. Just don't try `len(42)`—that'll throw a tantrum unless you convert it to a string first. Numbers don't like being measured by string rules. Python may be flexible, but even it draws the line somewhere.

8.

Now let's clean things up. The `strip()` method removes extra whitespace from both ends of a string:

```python
CopyEdit
```

```
name = "    Alice    "
cleaned = name.strip()
```
Poof—those unwanted spaces are gone. There's also `lstrip()` and `rstrip()` if you only want to trim one side. These are great for user input where people "accidentally" hold down the spacebar. Think of `strip()` as the lint roller for messy strings. Clean strings = clean code = happy coder.

9.

Strings come with their own set of built-in **methods**—like superpowers that only strings can use. Want to make everything lowercase? Try `"HELLO".lower()`. Want it uppercase? `"hello".upper()` delivers. Want to capitalize the first letter? Use `"python".capitalize()`. These methods don't mutate the original string—they return a new one. That's because strings in Python are **immutable**—once created, they can't be changed. Instead, you *create* new versions through operations. It's like remixing a song without touching the master recording.

10.

Checking if your string starts or ends with something? Say hello to `startswith()` and `endswith()`.

```python
CopyEdit
name = "Captain Code"
print(name.startswith("Cap"))    # True
print(name.endswith("Dog"))      # False
```
These are boolean-returning methods, perfect for conditionals and logic checks. You can even combine them with `if` statements to write witty validation rules. They're straightforward, readable, and oh-so-useful. Python wants you to succeed—and that means giving you methods that read like English.

11.

Let's get fancy with **find()** and **index()**. They help you locate substrings inside a larger string. `find()` returns the first position where the substring occurs or −1 if not found. `index()` does the same, but throws an error if it's not found—because it's dramatic like that. Example: `"banana".find("na")` gives 2. `"banana".index("na")` also gives 2, but `"banana".index("x")` raises an error. Use `find()` when you want safe, quiet failure. Use `index()` when you want to cause a scene.

12.

Replacing text is easy with `replace()`.

```python
CopyEdit
sentence = "Python is slow"
```

```python
new_sentence = sentence.replace("slow", "fast")
print(new_sentence)  # Python is fast
```
This creates a brand-new string with the swap in place. Like all string methods, it doesn't modify the original string. You can chain methods too: `sentence.replace("slow", "fast").upper()` becomes a confident shout. Want to remove a word entirely? Just replace it with an empty string: `.replace("boring", "")`. Editing strings is oddly satisfying—like digital wordsmithing.

13.

Want to split a string into a list? Use the `split()` method. `"one, two, three".split(", ")` becomes `['one', 'two', 'three']`. It defaults to splitting on spaces, but you can specify any delimiter. This is how you break sentences into words or CSV data into cells. You can even loop through the result:

python
CopyEdit
```python
for word in sentence.split():
    print(word)
```
Great for building search tools, filters, or chatbots that speak better than you do.

14.

Reversing a string isn't a method, but it's easy with slicing. `text[::-1]` flips the string backwards. `"Python"[::-1]` becomes `"nohtyP"`. Why does this work? The `[::-1]` slice tells Python to start at the end and move backward one step at a time. It's compact, clever, and perfect for palindromes. Want to check if a word reads the same forwards and backwards? Just compare it to its reverse. Python makes you look smart with minimal effort.

15.

String comparisons are case-sensitive by default. `"Python" == "python"` returns `False`. If you want a case-insensitive comparison, convert both sides to the same case:

python
CopyEdit
```python
a.lower() == b.lower()
```
This is especially useful for user input, where caps lock is a known saboteur. Always sanitize your strings when comparing. Trust no keyboard. People type weird things.

16.

Let's get a little artsy. You can **repeat** strings using multiplication: `"ha" * 3` gives `"hahaha"`. Combine this with variables and you've got mini-generators:

python
CopyEdit
```python
laugh = "ha"
```

```
echo = laugh * 5
print(echo)   # hahaha
```
This trick is oddly helpful in games, animations, or when writing "DON'T TOUCH THAT BUTTON" 20 times. Python doesn't judge. It just multiplies.

17.

Ever wanted to check if a word is *inside* a string? Use the `in` keyword:

```python
CopyEdit
"Py" in "Python"     # True
"snake" in "Python"  # False
```
This is a boolean expression—perfect for `if` statements. It's readable, expressive, and works with variables too. You'll use `in` a lot, whether searching, filtering, or verifying. Python syntax is practically poetry at this point. Haiku incoming.

18.

Sometimes you want multi-line strings—welcome to triple quotes. Use `"""` or `'''` to open a string that spans several lines:

```python
CopyEdit
poem = """Roses are red
Code can be neat
Python is friendly
And rarely offbeat."""
```
This is useful for documentation, email templates, or writing scripts that sound like bedtime stories. Python keeps the line breaks and indentation intact. Triple-quoted strings also double as multi-line comments when you're feeling rebellious. Just don't forget to close them.

19.

Let's challenge you. Create a script that takes your name and favorite food and returns: `"Hi NAME, I heard you like FOOD!"`. Use variables, f-strings, and at least one method like `.capitalize()` or `.upper()`. This will reinforce input, formatting, and structure. Make it quirky—your code should feel like *you*. Experiment with different styles, spacing, and separators. Add emojis if you're feeling spicy. Python won't mind—it likes flair.

20.

Remember: strings are the soul of your user experience. They greet your users, explain errors, display results, and even crack jokes (if you code them right). Treat them with care. Sanitize them, format them, and don't forget to spellcheck them. A single typo in a string can confuse a user—or make you look like you're drunk on semicolons. Strings carry your voice into the machine. And Python lets you speak clearly.

21.

So far, you've learned how to create, format, slice, search, modify, and multiply strings. You've wielded powerful methods and probably annoyed your friends with string-based jokes. You now have the skills to write programs that talk back—and sound good doing it. Whether you're building a chatbot, naming NPCs, or customizing error messages, strings are your secret sauce. Text is everywhere, and now you control it. With great strings come great responsibilities. And yes, that pun was intentional.

22.

In the next chapter, we'll dive into **Numbers**—Python's way of flexing its math muscles. Integers, floats, operators, and a few tricks involving decimals and rounding await. But for now, bask in the glow of your string mastery. Write something fun. Format it beautifully. Maybe even print a poem, a menu, or a fake fortune cookie. Because strings aren't just code—they're where code *starts talking*.

Chapter 4: Numbers Don't Lie – But They Might Divide Funny

1.

Let's be honest: numbers in programming are like onions—they have layers, they make people cry, and they're absolutely everywhere. From counting lives in a game to calculating mortgage payments, numbers are your loyal but occasionally confusing companions. Python handles numbers with grace, power, and just a hint of quirk. Whether you're dealing with whole numbers or decimal drama, Python has a type for it. In this chapter, we'll dive deep into integers, floats, math operations, and even the dark arts of rounding. Because while numbers don't lie, they do occasionally round in unexpected directions. And heaven help you if you confuse integer division with float division. Ready to crunch?

2.

First up: **integers**, or `int` for short. These are your plain ol' whole numbers—positive, negative, or zero. Think `1`, `-5`, `42`, and your shoe size (probably). Python makes it absurdly easy to assign them: `age = 35`, `points = -1000`. Want to verify the type? Just run `type(age)` and Python will proudly announce `<class 'int'>`. Integers are great for counting, indexing, and arguing over who scored more. They don't do decimals. They're confident in their wholeness.

3.

Next in line: **floats**, short for "floating-point numbers," because apparently programmers hate normal names. Floats include decimal points—`3.14`, `-0.001`, `100.0`. Assigning one is as easy as sneezing: `pi = 3.14159`. Python recognizes it instantly as a float. You can always convert an integer to a float using `float(5)` which becomes `5.0`. Floats are used in calculations that require precision—money, measurements, physics simulations, or dividing pizza fairly. But beware: floats come with caveats. More on that in a moment.

4.

Let's talk math—the kind even your calculator would envy. Python supports all the basic operators: `+`, `-`, `*`, `/`, `%`, `**`, and `//`. Addition, subtraction, multiplication, and division are exactly what you expect. The `%` is called the **modulus**, and it gives you the *remainder* of a division. Try `10 % 3`, and you'll get `1`. `**` is for exponentiation: `2 ** 3` equals `8`. And `//` is **floor division**—it divides and drops the decimals like a stoic monk. More on that spicy operator soon.

5.

Let's practice:

```python
CopyEdit
a = 10
b = 3
print(a + b)     # 13
print(a - b)     # 7
print(a * b)     # 30
print(a / b)     # 3.333...
print(a % b)     # 1
print(a ** b)    # 1000
print(a // b)    # 3
```

Look at you—calculating like a Python-powered genius. Just don't divide by zero. Python hates that.

6.

About that divide-by-zero thing. If you attempt `10 / 0`, Python won't quietly hand you infinity like a chill math professor. Instead, you get:

```python
CopyEdit
ZeroDivisionError: division by zero
```

Because dividing by zero breaks the laws of both math and physics. It's not Python being rude—it's protecting you from the void. So always check before dividing: `if b != 0:` is your friend. A quick conditional check saves you from crashing your program and your soul.

7.

Now let's talk **float weirdness**, because it's real and it's everywhere. Try this: `print(0.1 + 0.2)` and you might expect `0.3`. But Python returns `0.30000000000000004`—a digital burp caused by how computers store decimals in binary. It's not a bug, it's a *feature*... of how floating-point arithmetic works. Computers store floats in base-2, not base-10, which causes tiny inaccuracies. For most tasks, you'll never notice. But if you're doing financial calculations or launching rockets, use the `decimal` module. It's precision for the perfectionist.

8.

Let's tame those decimals with **rounding**. The `round()` function helps you keep things tidy: `round(3.14159, 2)` gives `3.14`. You can round to zero decimal places: `round(3.7)` returns `4`. It even follows "round half to even" in edge cases—also known as **bankers' rounding**. This reduces rounding bias in big datasets, but can be surprising at first. Try `round(2.5)` and `round(3.5)`—you'll get `2` and `4`. That's Python trying to be fair, not flaky. And yes, you can override it with custom logic if needed.

9.

Type conversion is how Python avoids becoming a math snob. You can convert `int` to `float`, `float` to `int`, and even numbers to strings. `int(3.9)` returns `3`—no rounding, just chopping. `float(7)` gives `7.0`, and `str(42)` gives `"42"`. This is super useful when mixing numbers and text. Just remember: you can't convert `"hello"` to an integer without triggering an existential crisis. Try converting only when it makes logical sense. Python's flexible, but not telepathic.

10.

Let's take a closer look at **floor division**. The `//` operator divides two numbers but *discards* the decimal. `7 // 2` returns `3`, not `3.5`. This is great when you want whole-number results without rounding up. It's perfect for things like counting how many pizzas you can buy without going over budget. If you want the leftover money, use the modulus `%`. Between `//` and `%`, you can split and remainder your way through life like a budget-savvy wizard. Math has never felt this practical.

11.

Need math functions? Python's `math` module is a gold mine. Import it with `import math` and unlock `math.sqrt()`, `math.ceil()`, `math.floor()`, `math.pi`, and more. Try `math.sqrt(16)` for square roots or `math.ceil(4.3)` to round *up*. `math.floor(4.7)` rounds *down*, like a pessimistic realist. There's even `math.pow(2, 3)`—though `2 ** 3` works just as well. The `math` module is your friend when Python's basic operators aren't quite enough. It's got sine, cosine, and other fancy functions too.

12.

Let's do a real-world example. Say you're splitting a bill:

```python
CopyEdit
total = 75.25
people = 3
each = total / people
```

```
print(f"Each pays: ${round(each, 2)}")
```
This script uses floats, division, and rounding in one graceful swoop. Real-world math is messy, but Python makes it manageable. You can expand this to include tax, tip, or angry friends who don't believe in math. Suddenly, you're writing a mini app—and it all started with numbers.

13.

Variables and math are like peanut butter and jelly. You can store your calculations in variables:

python
CopyEdit
```
subtotal = 50
tax = subtotal * 0.07
total = subtotal + tax
```
Now you've built a receipt calculator. Changing `subtotal` updates everything—because math is dynamic, not static. This is where programming shines over calculators. Your code adapts. And you look brilliant.

14.

Python even respects **operator precedence**. That means multiplication and division happen before addition and subtraction. So `5 + 2 * 3` equals `11`, not `21`. Want to override that? Use parentheses: `(5 + 2) * 3` equals `21`. Python follows the PEMDAS order just like you learned in school. Yes, that traumatic acronym lives on. But now you're the one in control.

15.

Need randomness? Import `random`.

python
CopyEdit
```
import random
dice = random.randint(1, 6)
```
Just like that, you've rolled a digital die. You can generate random floats, shuffle lists, and simulate chaos with Python's blessing. Use randomness in games, simulations, or when choosing what to eat. Life is unpredictable—your code can be too.

16.

Want to format numbers? Try `format()` or f-strings with specifiers.

python
CopyEdit
```
score = 99.456
print(f"Score: {score:.2f}")   # Score: 99.46
```
The `.2f` says "two decimal places, please." You can also pad numbers with zeros: `f"{7:03}"` gives `"007"`. Great for printing tables, IDs, or Bond intros. Formatting makes your numbers look professional, even if your code is powered by coffee and chaos.

17.

Let's not forget about booleans in math. You can do weird stuff like: `True + True` equals 2. That's because Python treats `True` as 1 and `False` as 0. Useful for counting conditions or scoring tests:

```python
CopyEdit
score = (answer1 == "A") + (answer2 == "B")
```
It's clever, compact, and just a little cheeky. Python's logic doesn't just check—it counts.

18.

Here's a fun trick: chaining math and strings.

```python
CopyEdit
stars = "*" * 10
print(stars)   # **********
```
Yes, you multiplied a string with a number—and it worked. Try building a bar chart using numbers and symbols. Suddenly, you're turning math into art. Who said left-brainers can't be creative?

19.

Here's your challenge: write a script that asks the user for two numbers, adds them, and prints the result. Then subtract, multiply, and divide them too. Use `input()`, convert to `float()`, and use f-strings to print results. Add rounding and a witty message at the end. Now you've built a calculator. Next step: world domination. Or at least an A+ in Python 101.

20.

Let's recap: you've explored integers, floats, operators, rounding, type conversion, and the math module. You've used math in real-world examples, made numbers talk, and dodged divide-by-zero disasters. You've learned to respect the precision of floats and the usefulness of formatting. Python gives you the tools; you bring the logic. From here, math only gets cooler. Especially when we mix it with conditionals. Spoiler alert: that's what's next.

21.

Remember, math in Python is not just about calculators. It's about creating systems, building logic, and making decisions. Numbers drive everything from scoring apps to simulations to space launches. With Python, you're not just crunching numbers—you're commanding them. Math becomes your language. Python is the translator. Together, you're unstoppable.

22.

In the next chapter, we'll explore **Booleans and Conditionals**—the decision-makers of the Python world. You'll learn how to write programs that can think, choose, and respond. It's where logic comes alive, and where your code starts branching like a choose-your-own-adventure novel. For now, give yourself a high-five—you've conquered the numbers. Even the ones that divide funny.

Chapter 5: Booleans & Conditionals – Making Decisions Without Regret

1.
Welcome to the thinking part of your Python journey. Up until now, your code has just done what you told it—no questions asked, no judgment passed. But real programs need choices, forks in the road, and sometimes dramatic ultimatums. Enter **Booleans** and **conditionals**—Python's way of giving your code a brain and a bit of sass. Booleans are the digital versions of *yes* and *no*, encoded as `True` and `False` (capitalized because Python has standards). Conditionals let your code ask, "Should I?" and "What if?" and "Are we really doing this?" Think of Booleans as binary lights—on or off, go or stop. And conditionals as the decision tree that guides the journey.

2.
Let's meet the Boolean stars of the show: `True` and `False`. These aren't strings; they're actual built-in constants. You can assign them to variables like `is_hungry = True` or `is_sleeping = False`. You can print them, compare them, and treat them like tiny one-bit philosophers. In math, `True` is 1 and `False` is 0, which means `True + True` equals 2 (yes, seriously). This becomes surprisingly useful in scoring and decision trees. You can use `type(True)` and see that it's a `<class 'bool'>`. Python doesn't just let you write conditions—it *lives* for them.

3.
Now onto conditionals—the mighty `if` statement. The syntax is beautiful in its simplicity:

```python
CopyEdit
if condition:
    do_something()
```

Replace `condition` with a Boolean expression, and `do_something()` will run only if it evaluates to `True`. For example:

```python
CopyEdit
if is_hungry:
    print("Time for snacks!")
```

If `is_hungry` is `True`, Python delivers the snacks. Otherwise, it skips the buffet entirely.

4.
Let's add more choices with `else`. It's the code that runs when your `if` condition is `False`. Like this:

```python
CopyEdit
if is_hungry:
    print("Eat food.")
else:
    print("Do something productive.")
```
Think of `else` as the fallback plan, the backup parachute. Python evaluates the `if`, and if that doesn't fly, it jumps to `else`. It's logic with a contingency plan. No regrets, just reroutes.

5.

Need more options? That's where `elif` (short for "else if") steps in. It's Python's way of saying, "Not that, but maybe this?" Here's how it looks:

```python
CopyEdit
if mood == "happy":
    print("Smile!")
elif mood == "sad":
    print("Hug a cat.")
else:
    print("Check your caffeine levels.")
```
Python checks each condition in order, top to bottom. The first one that's `True` wins—like logic bingo. Only one block runs, so prioritize your conditions wisely.

6.

Let's break down comparisons—the tools that fuel these decisions. Python supports `==` (equals), `!=` (not equal), `>`, `<`, `>=`, and `<=`. Notice that `==` is double equals—not to be confused with `=`, which assigns values. `if age == 18:` checks if someone is 18. `if age != 18:` checks if they are **not**. These comparisons return Booleans: either `True` or `False`. That's all your `if` statement needs to function. Boolean expressions are the currency of conditional logic.

7.

Python also supports **logical operators**: `and`, `or`, and `not`. These let you combine Boolean expressions like a logic DJ.

```python
CopyEdit
if is_tired and is_hungry:
    print("Nap with snacks.")
```
`and` means both conditions must be true. `or` means either can be true. `not` flips the logic—`not True` is `False`, and vice versa. These allow you to create layered, complex conditions without needing caffeine-fueled flowcharts.

8.

Want to see how Python interprets truthiness? It treats certain values as `False`: `0`, `None`, empty strings (`" "`), empty lists (`[ ]`), empty dicts (`{ }`), and `False` itself. Everything else is `True`. So `if "hello":` will run, but `if " ":` will not. Same goes for numbers: `if 0:` is falsey, but `if 5:` is truthy. You can test this with `bool(value)`. Python's Boolean lens is surprisingly intuitive. It's not just about `True` and `False`—it's about what *feels* true.

9.

Let's get practical. Ask for user input and make a decision:

```python
CopyEdit
age = int(input("Enter your age: "))
if age >= 18:
    print("You're an adult.")
else:
    print("Not quite there yet.")
```
This is real-world logic based on user data. You've combined input, type conversion, comparison, and a decision tree. All in a few lines of Python. That's the power of conditionals. And the gateway to smarter programs.

10.

Nested conditionals are totally allowed. You can put an `if` inside another `if` like so:

```python
CopyEdit
if logged_in:
    if is_admin:
        print("Welcome, Commander.")
```
But be careful—too many nested levels can lead to logic spaghetti. Python thrives on clarity. Use logical operators (`and, or`) to flatten where you can. Nest when necessary, but indent with care. Deep nesting leads to tears and lost weekend hours.

11.

Let's say you want to check multiple conditions against one value. Instead of repeating yourself, use `in`.

```python
CopyEdit
if mood in ["happy", "excited", "motivated"]:
    print("Great time to code!")
```

The `in` keyword checks membership in a list, string, or other iterable. It's compact, elegant, and expressive. Much cleaner than writing `if mood == "happy" or mood == "excited"`... you get the idea. Lists make logic look good.

12.

Sometimes you just need to skip or pass. That's what `pass` is for.

```python
CopyEdit
if condition:
    pass  # to be implemented later
```

It tells Python, "Yes, this block exists, but I'm not ready yet." It's a placeholder, not a performer. Great for scaffolding your logic while your ideas catch up. It also stops Python from throwing an `IndentationError` tantrum.

13.

The `is` keyword checks identity, not equality. For example: `if item is None:` is how you check for a lack of value. Don't confuse it with `==`, which compares values. `is` compares object identities—whether two variables point to the same place in memory. It's subtle, but important. Especially when working with `None`, booleans, or singletons. Just remember: use `is` when you care about *who*, and `==` when you care about *what*.

14.

Short-circuiting is Python's way of being efficient. In an `or` statement, if the first condition is `True`, Python doesn't bother checking the rest. In an `and` statement, if the first condition is `False`, it skips the rest. Why waste cycles when you already know the outcome? This can save time, especially with functions or large datasets. It also means your second condition won't run if it doesn't have to. Python's lazy—but in a smart way.

15.

Ternary expressions let you write quick decisions in a single line.

```python
CopyEdit
message = "Adult" if age >= 18 else "Minor"
```

This is a clean, readable way to assign based on a condition. It's compact and expressive—great for simple logic. But don't go cramming whole novels into a ternary. If it looks like a puzzle, go back to full `if/else`. One-liners are cool, but clarity is cooler.

16.

Booleans play nicely with numbers. Since `True == 1` and `False == 0`, you can use them in arithmetic.

```python
```

```
score = (guess == answer) + bonus
```

Or tally up `True` results in a list:

```
results = [True, False, True]
print(sum(results))   # 2
```

It's Boolean sorcery for counting correct answers, passes, or checkboxes. Clean. Clever. Pythonic.

17.

Booleans are also great for controlling **flow**. For example, keep asking for input **while** a condition is `True`:

```
while user_input != "exit":
    user_input = input("Type 'exit' to quit: ")
```

You've now entered the realm of *control structures*, where Booleans steer the ship. The `while` loop is basically a Boolean-fueled engine. We'll dive deeper into loops soon. For now, just know that logic flows where Booleans point.

18.

Here's a mini program to test your decision-making:

```
temp = int(input("What's the temperature? "))
if temp > 90:
    print("It's scorching! Stay inside.")
elif temp > 70:
    print("Perfect weather!")
elif temp > 50:
    print("Mild. Maybe bring a jacket.")
else:
    print("Bundle up. It's chilly.")
```

This script makes decisions based on ranges—classic conditional territory. Small code, big brains.

19.

Ready for a trick? Python lets you chain comparisons like math class:

```
if 18 <= age < 65:
    print("You're of working age.")
```

This is more readable than writing `age >= 18 and age < 65`. It's elegant, accurate, and very Pythonic. Use it to make your logic more expressive. Python loves when code reads like English. So does your future self.

20.

Let's recap what you've conquered. You've met Booleans, conditionals, comparison operators, logical operators, and ternary expressions. You've built decision trees and written code that *thinks*. Python is no longer a one-track machine—it makes choices based on your logic. That's power. That's control. That's progress.

21.

Now that your code can make decisions, it's time to **repeat itself**—intentionally. Loops are the next milestone. They allow you to automate tasks, iterate over data, and repeat actions without writing the same line 100 times. If conditionals are your brain, loops are your muscle memory. In the next chapter, we'll make your code do some cardio.

22.

So take a bow—you've learned to think in Python. You can ask questions, evaluate truth, and take different paths based on logic. You've tamed the two-headed Boolean beast and lived to tell the tale. Next stop: **Loops**—where repetition meets elegance and your keyboard finally gets a break.

Chapter 6: Loops – Repeating Yourself Elegantly

1.

Welcome to the land of **loops**, where repetition isn't just allowed—it's *celebrated*. Loops are Python's way of saying, "Let's do that again... and again... and again," without copying and pasting your code into oblivion. If conditionals let your code make decisions, loops let it develop *habits*. Think of loops like playlists on repeat—once Python hits play, it keeps going until the conditions say, "That's enough." Whether you're processing data, printing patterns, or asking the user to stop hitting Enter, loops have your back. They're the heart of automation, the soul of iteration, and the reason your fingers don't fall off writing redundant lines. Without loops, coding would be one long déjà vu. Let's end that madness—elegantly.

2.

Python gives you two primary loops: `while` and `for`. They each have their specialty, like the Batman and Robin of repetition. The `while` loop repeats *as long as a condition is true*. The `for` loop iterates *over a sequence*, like a list or range. They both let you reuse logic without repeating yourself manually. Each loop has different vibes—`while` is more rebellious and unpredictable; `for` is clean and dependable. But both will save your sanity and impress your coworkers. And possibly your cat.

3.

Let's meet `while` first. Its structure is simple:

python
CopyEdit
```python
while condition:
    do_something()
```
Python checks the condition—if it's `True`, it runs the code block, then checks again. If it's `False`, it stops. You can loop forever if you're not careful. For example:

python
CopyEdit
```python
while True:
    print("Forever coding...")
```
Press Ctrl+C to escape before your monitor catches fire.

4.

Here's a classic `while` loop with an exit plan:

python
CopyEdit
```python
count = 0
while count < 5:
    print(f"Count is {count}")
    count += 1
```
This prints values from 0 to 4, then stops when `count` hits 5. Without `count += 1`, you'd be stuck in a loop until retirement. Incrementing (or decrementing) your control variable is essential. Python doesn't guess your exit strategy—you have to tell it. Every loop deserves a graceful way out.

5.

Now, let's bring in `for`. It's made for walking through sequences.

python
CopyEdit
```python
for number in [1, 2, 3]:
    print(number)
```
This loop runs three times—once for each item in the list. Python assigns each value to `number`, then runs the indented block. No need to manage an index, increment anything, or

break out the abacus. `for` is tidy, intuitive, and versatile. It's the loop you take home to meet your parents.

6.

Tired of writing lists by hand? Python's got you: `range()` generates sequences for loops.

python
```python
for i in range(5):
    print(i)
```
This prints numbers from 0 to 4. The default `range(n)` goes from 0 up to—but not including —n. You can also pass two arguments: `range(start, stop)`, or three: `range(start, stop, step)`. For example, `range(1, 10, 2)` gives you all odd numbers from 1 to 9. Python's built-in number wizard saves the day.

7.

Need a countdown? Reverse that `range`:

python
```python
for i in range(5, 0, -1):
    print(i)
```
That third argument is your **step**, and a negative step goes backwards. You can countdown to liftoff or loop through anything in reverse. Python doesn't care—it just follows instructions like a loyal minion. Want to loop infinitely with `for`? You can't—unless you're looping over an infinite generator. We'll get there eventually. For now, `range()` is plenty powerful.

8.

Let's add control: `break` and `continue` are loop lifesavers. `break` ends the loop immediately, even if the condition isn't false yet.

python
```python
for num in range(10):
    if num == 5:
        break
    print(num)
```
This prints 0 to 4, then stops. `continue` skips the current iteration and moves on. Great for filtering, skipping bad data, or dodging weird inputs.

9.

Example with `continue`:

python

```python
for num in range(5):
    if num == 2:
        continue
    print(num)
```

This skips printing 2 but prints the others. Python doesn't get mad—it just moves on. Think of `continue` as a diplomatic way to say, "No thanks, next." It's great for ignoring errors, skipping blank inputs, or just being picky. Code with standards.

10.

Let's add some flair. Want to track progress? Try:

python
```python
for i in range(1, 6):
    print(f"Step {i}/5...")
```
This gives your loop a progress narrative. Add a sleep delay with `time.sleep(1)` (after `import time`) for dramatic effect. Suddenly, you're not just looping—you're telling a story. Users appreciate visual feedback. Loops can entertain and inform.

11.

Python lets you loop through any iterable: lists, tuples, strings, dictionaries, even files.

python
```python
for char in "Python":
    print(char)
```
This prints each character on a new line. Strings are iterable, meaning Python will break them down letter by letter. You can also loop through lists of names, shopping items, or quests. Anything that's iterable is loop-friendly. Python loves patterns.

12.

Looping through dictionaries requires finesse.

python
```python
person = {"name": "Alice", "age": 30}
for key in person:
    print(key, person[key])
```
Want more control? Use `.items()`:

python
```python
for key, value in person.items():
```

```python
    print(f"{key}: {value}")
```
This unpacks each key-value pair for cleaner access. Dictionaries are like mini databases—and loops are your data tour guides.

13.

Let's tackle **nested loops**—a loop within a loop.

```python
CopyEdit
for i in range(3):
    for j in range(2):
        print(f"i={i}, j={j}")
```
Useful for grids, combinations, and anything two-dimensional. But beware: they multiply quickly. Three nested loops? You're officially in loop inception. Indent wisely and keep your logic clean.

14.

Sometimes you want to do something *after* a loop finishes. Python's got a rare gem: the `else` clause on loops.

```python
CopyEdit
for num in range(3):
    print(num)
else:
    print("Loop complete!")
```
It only runs if the loop ends naturally—not if it's `break`-interrupted. It's like a final bow after a performance. Most people don't know it exists. Now you're in the loop elite.

15.

Looping with `enumerate()` lets you track indexes without manual counting.

```python
CopyEdit
for index, item in enumerate(["a", "b", "c"]):
    print(f"{index}: {item}")
```
No need for `range(len(list))`. Python handles both the value and its position for you. Clean, readable, and very Pythonic. Loop smarter, not harder.

16.

Want to zip through two lists at once? Use `zip()`.

```python
CopyEdit
```

```python
names = ["Alice", "Bob"]
scores = [95, 87]
for name, score in zip(names, scores):
    print(f"{name} scored {score}")
```

`zip()` pairs up items into tuples. Great for spreadsheets, reports, or syncing data. It stops at the shortest list, so keep lengths equal for best results.

17.
Let's automate with style:

```python
CopyEdit
tasks = ["code", "debug", "test", "repeat"]
for task in tasks:
    print(f"Now: {task.upper()}")
```

You've looped, transformed, and printed—all in one go. You could even build to-do lists, progress trackers, or motivational bots. Python doesn't just loop—it delivers.

18.
Here's your mission: build a loop that counts down from 10 and prints "LIFTOFF!" at the end. Use `range()`, a `for` loop, and maybe `time.sleep(1)` for drama. Bonus points if you add sound effects with `"*boom*"` or emojis. Use loops to build excitement. Automation can be theatrical. Why not?

19.
Recap time! You've learned `while`, `for`, `break`, `continue`, `range`, `zip`, `enumerate`, and more. You can loop through lists, strings, dictionaries, and nested data. You now know how to control the loop flow like a conductor with a baton made of logic. Python's looping tools are precise, powerful, and poetic. And you've just scratched the surface. Next chapter: you build structures.

20.
Why are loops so powerful? Because they let you *scale*. One line inside a loop can process a hundred items. You write logic once, and Python applies it again and again. That's the essence of programming: write once, reuse infinitely. Loops make your code efficient, elegant, and effective. Without them, your program is just a to-do list. With them? It's a full-blown productivity machine.

21.
With loops mastered, you're ready to explore **collections**—starting with **lists**, the grocery bags of Python. They're mutable, flexible, and wonderfully iterable. In the next chapter, we'll fill lists, sort them, slice them, and mutate them like digital gene editing. You'll love them. You may even name a few. Lists are life.

22.

So take a victory lap—on repeat, naturally. You've just leveled up in Python by learning to automate repetition with elegance. Whether you're looping through strings, data, or dance moves, Python is with you every step of the way. Next stop: **Lists – The Grocery Bag of Python**. Pack wisely. We're going shopping.

Chapter 7: Lists – The Grocery Bag of Python

1.

Imagine needing to carry multiple values—numbers, strings, maybe a llama emoji. Instead of juggling a dozen variables like a sleep-deprived circus act, Python offers a much better solution: **lists**. Lists are Python's way of bundling things—like a grocery bag that holds apples, bread, and questionable life decisions. They can store anything: numbers, strings, other lists, or even functions if you're feeling extra. And unlike strings, lists are *mutable*, meaning you can add, remove, and rearrange their contents without needing a whole new bag. Lists maintain order, allow duplicates, and politely follow whatever you ask them to do (mostly). They're one of the most used data structures in Python—and for good reason. So grab your cart, because we're going list shopping.

2.

Creating a list is as simple as wrapping items in square brackets.

python
CopyEdit
```python
groceries = ["milk", "eggs", "bread"]
```
Each item is separated by a comma and maintains its order. You can print it, loop through it, and even access specific items using indices. Try `print(groceries[0])` and you'll see `"milk"`. Like strings, lists are zero-indexed—meaning the first item is at position `0`, not `1`. Negative indices work too: `groceries[-1]` gives you `"bread"`. Lists are organized, polite, and a little bit flexible.

3.

Lists can hold *anything*. Numbers, booleans, strings, even other lists.

python
CopyEdit
```python
mixed = [42, "hello", True, [1, 2, 3]]
```

You can even mix types without Python blinking. It's like a digital junk drawer, and Python's fine with it. But just because you *can* mix everything doesn't mean you *should*. Homogeneous lists (same-type items) are easier to manage in the long run. Still, the flexibility is there when you need it. Python trusts your organizational instincts.

4.

Let's talk **indexing**. Want the second item in your list? Use `my_list[1]`. Want the last? `my_list[-1]`. Want to assign a new value? You can! `my_list[0] = "cheese"` replaces `"milk"` with `"cheese"` like a grocery plot twist. Indexing is your way of reaching in and pulling out exactly what you need. But be careful not to ask for an index that doesn't exist — it'll throw an `IndexError` faster than you can say "out of bounds." Check `len(my_list)` before poking around.

5.

Speaking of **length**, the `len()` function tells you how many items are in your list.

```python
CopyEdit
len(groceries)
```

This is handy for loops, checks, and bragging about how many types of pasta you hoard. Use it often — it's your list's built-in measuring tape. And since lists are dynamic, `len()` updates automatically as you add or remove items. It's like having a digital pedometer for your data. Python keeps count so you don't have to.

6.

Adding items is easy with `append()`.

```python
CopyEdit
groceries.append("butter")
```

This adds `"butter"` to the end of the list. You can keep adding more like it's a buffet line. Want to insert something in a specific position? Use `insert(index, item)`:

```python
CopyEdit
groceries.insert(1, "coffee")
```

Now `"coffee"` lives at position 1, and everything else shifts right. Python's list is flexible like a yogi.

7.

Need to remove something? You've got options. Use `remove(value)` to delete the first matching item:

```python
CopyEdit
```

```python
groceries.remove("eggs")
```
Or use `pop(index)` to yank an item by its position—`groceries.pop(0)` removes the first. Calling `pop()` without arguments removes the last item. It's great for stack-like behavior, like undoing tasks. You can also use `del groceries[2]` to remove an item without ceremony. When you want a clean house, Python hands you the broom.

8.
Sometimes you just want to **clear** the whole list.

python
CopyEdit
```python
groceries.clear()
```
Poof—empty list. It's still there, just… empty. Perfect when you need to reset or reuse the variable. Think of it as a digital CTRL+Z. Just make sure you don't need the data anymore—it's a one-way trip.

9.
Want to copy a list? Be careful—`new_list = old_list` doesn't actually copy it; it just points to the same list. Changing `new_list` will also change `old_list`. Instead, use `.copy()` or slicing:

python
CopyEdit
```python
new_list = old_list.copy()
# or
new_list = old_list[:]
```
Now you've got a brand-new list, not just a different name for the same one. Python references are sneaky like that.

10.
Lists support **slicing**, just like strings.

python
CopyEdit
```python
groceries[1:3]
```
This gives a sublist starting at index 1 and ending *before* index 3. Leave out the start to begin at the beginning: `groceries[:2]`. Leave out the end to go to the finish: `groceries[2:]`. Use negative indices to slice from the end: `groceries[-3:]`. You can even use steps: `groceries[::2]` gives every other item. It's like a buffet line with a secret pattern.

11.
Sorting is simple with `.sort()`.

python

```
names = ["Charlie", "Alice", "Bob"]
names.sort()
print(names)  # ['Alice', 'Bob', 'Charlie']
```

By default, Python sorts in ascending order. For descending, use `names.sort(reverse=True)`. Want to sort without changing the original list? Use `sorted(names)` instead. That's the non-destructive way to organize. Python gives you both options—neat freak or minimalist chaos.

12.

Let's loop through a list:

python

```
for item in groceries:
    print(f"Don't forget: {item}")
```

This prints each item one at a time. Lists and loops go together like peanut butter and syntax. Whether you're printing, filtering, or processing items, looping is the gateway to control. Pair it with `enumerate()` and you even get the index:

python

```
for index, item in enumerate(groceries):
    print(f"{index}: {item}")
```

Efficiency meets elegance.

13.

Want to check if an item is in the list? Use the `in` keyword:

python

```
if "milk" in groceries:
    print("We're stocked!")
```

It returns `True` or `False`, depending on the presence of the item. This is great for filters, validations, and being just a little judgy. You can also use `not in` to flip it. Python keeps it natural—almost like English.

14.

Lists can be joined or extended. Use `+` to combine:

python

```
combined = groceries + snacks
```

This makes a new list with everything from both. Or use `.extend()` to add all items from another list:

```python
CopyEdit
groceries.extend(["jam", "tea"])
```

The original list grows longer without nesting. Choose based on whether you want a new list or to grow an existing one. Python is flexible with your shopping habits.

15.

List comprehensions are like list-making superpowers.

```python
CopyEdit
squares = [x * x for x in range(10)]
```

This one-liner creates a list of squares from 0 to 9. You can even filter it:

```python
CopyEdit
evens = [x for x in range(10) if x % 2 == 0]
```

List comprehensions are fast, readable, and oddly satisfying. They're like Python poetry — efficient and expressive.

16.

Let's go wild: lists *within* lists.

```python
CopyEdit
matrix = [[1, 2], [3, 4], [5, 6]]
```

Access them like this: `matrix[0][1]` gives 2. It's like coordinates in a spreadsheet. You can loop through rows and then through columns. Nested lists are perfect for grids, maps, or spreadsheet-like structures. But watch your brackets — double indexing gets tricky fast.

17.

Let's do some counting.

```python
CopyEdit
numbers = [1, 2, 3, 2, 4, 2]
print(numbers.count(2))   # 3
```

`.count(value)` returns how many times a value appears. Want to find the index of the first occurrence? Use `.index(value)`. These are handy for analysis, validation, or just figuring out who invited "cheese" to the list three times.

18.

Lists don't have to be static. You can build them on the fly.

```python
CopyEdit
items = []
items.append("start")
```

Now you've got a growing container. Add items based on user input, conditions, or loops. Build your list as the program runs. Python encourages dynamic thinking.

19.

Your mini-project: write a to-do list app. Ask the user for 5 tasks, one by one. Append each to a list. Then print them out as a checklist with numbers:

```python
CopyEdit
1. Wash dishes
2. Water plants
3. Learn Python
```

This reinforces input, loops, and list manipulation. Bonus points if you add the ability to remove items later.

20.

Let's recap. Lists are ordered, mutable, and iterable. You can index, slice, sort, copy, and loop through them with ease. You can append, extend, remove, and build dynamically. They play nicely with loops, conditions, and comprehensions. They're Python's favorite utility belt. And by now, they should be yours too.

21.

Lists are one of the most powerful tools in Python. Whether you're storing groceries, user data, or a thousand spaceship names, lists make it elegant and effortless. They grow with you, adapt to your needs, and perform with grace. You've unlocked a fundamental skill—and one you'll use in nearly every project. The more you use them, the more versatile they become. Python's philosophy is "batteries included," and lists are one of its juiciest batteries.

22.

Next up: **Dictionaries – Keys, Values, and Chaos Organized**. Because sometimes a list isn't enough—you need labeled data. You'll learn to associate names with values, organize information, and create your own miniature databases. For now, give yourself a round of applause—you've earned it. Your grocery bag is full. Let's unpack some dictionaries next.

Chapter 8: Dictionaries – Keys, Values, and Chaos Organized

1.

Picture this: you have a list of items, but you keep forgetting what each one means. Is "Bob" a name, a role, or your neighbor's Wi-Fi password? You need structure, labels, and a little order in the chaos. Enter **dictionaries**, Python's way of pairing things up like a matchmaking service for data. A dictionary maps **keys** to **values**, just like a real dictionary maps words to definitions. Except here, "name" might map to "Alice", and "age" might map to 30. Lists are great for ordered collections, but dictionaries are built for **meaning**. They turn unstructured data into something you can actually use.

2.

Let's start with syntax.

```python
CopyEdit
person = {"name": "Alice", "age": 30, "job": "Engineer"}
```

Keys are on the left, values on the right, separated by colons and wrapped in curly braces. Each pair is called a **key-value pair**. You can think of it as a miniature database—structured, labeled, and instantly accessible. Python doesn't require all values to be the same type either—you can mix strings, numbers, lists, even other dictionaries. The key must be **immutable** (strings, numbers, or tuples), but the value can be anything your heart desires. Just don't use lists or other dicts as keys—Python draws the line at chaos *that* deep.

3.

Accessing values is like looking up definitions.

```python
CopyEdit
print(person["name"])  # Alice
```

You use the key inside square brackets, and Python returns the matching value. Try using a key that doesn't exist, and Python will explode with a **KeyError**. You can avoid that with **.get()**:

```python
CopyEdit
print(person.get("salary"))  # None
```

Or provide a backup value: **person.get("salary", "Not specified")**. It's polite, graceful, and prevents your program from turning into a flaming wreck.

4.

Want to add a new entry? Easy.

```python
CopyEdit
person["salary"] = 75000
```

Want to update an existing one? Same process. If the key exists, its value changes; if not, Python creates it. You don't need a special function—it's that simple. You can even overwrite values:

```python
CopyEdit
person["job"] = "Senior Engineer"
```

Python just nods and moves on.

5.

To remove entries, use `del`.

```python
CopyEdit
del person["salary"]
```

The key and its value vanish instantly. Or use `.pop(key)` to both remove and retrieve the value:

```python
CopyEdit
age = person.pop("age")
```

Perfect if you want to delete with dignity. There's also `.clear()` to wipe the whole dictionary. Useful during existential crises or data resets.

6.

Let's loop through a dictionary.

```python
CopyEdit
for key in person:
    print(f"{key}: {person[key]}")
```

This gives you each key and its corresponding value. Want both together, nicely unpacked? Use `.items()`:

```python
CopyEdit
for key, value in person.items():
    print(f"{key} => {value}")
```

This is Python's way of handing you both pieces at once, like a parent serving pizza *and* soda.

7.

Want just the keys or just the values? Python's got you.

```python
CopyEdit
print(person.keys())    # dict_keys(['name', 'job'])
print(person.values())  # dict_values(['Alice', 'Senior
Engineer'])
```

These look like lists, but they're actually **views**—dynamic windows into the dictionary. They update automatically if the dictionary changes. Convert them to lists with `list(person.keys())` if needed. It's like putting a view into a shopping cart.

8.

Dictionaries don't allow duplicate keys. If you try this:

```python
CopyEdit
data = {"a": 1, "a": 2}
```

The second `"a"` overwrites the first. No error, no warning—just silent replacement. So be mindful when creating dictionaries. Every key must be unique. Values can repeat, but keys must stay in their own lane.

9.

Dictionaries are perfect for **lookups**. Say you want to translate `"cat"` to `"gato"` in Spanish:

```python
CopyEdit
translate = {"cat": "gato", "dog": "perro"}
print(translate["cat"])  # gato
```

Boom—instant translator. This is how dictionaries power everything from word lookups to routing systems to game inventories. Whenever you need quick access by a label or ID, think dictionaries.

10.

Let's build a small phone book:

```python
CopyEdit
contacts = {
    "Alice": "555-1234",
    "Bob": "555-5678"
}
print(contacts["Bob"])
```

Now your Python program can call people—digitally, at least. Add, update, and remove contacts on the fly. With a loop, you can even print them alphabetically using `sorted(contacts)`. Python turns your data into a social butterfly.

11.

Nested dictionaries? Oh yes, it's a thing.

```python
CopyEdit
users = {
    "alice": {"age": 30, "email": "alice@example.com"},
    "bob": {"age": 25, "email": "bob@example.com"}
}
print(users["bob"]["email"])
```
This is a dictionary inside a dictionary—a hierarchy of info. Great for storing users, products, profiles, and even dragons. You can loop through them with nested loops, but brace yourself—it's bracket city.

12.

Need to check if a key exists? Use `in`:

```python
CopyEdit
if "age" in person:
    print("Age found!")
```
This is cleaner than handling a `KeyError`. Python doesn't mind peeking first. You can also check values, though that requires `value in dict.values()`. Don't confuse checking keys with checking values—they're on different sides of the colon.

13.

Want to merge two dictionaries? Use `.update()`:

```python
CopyEdit
new_info = {"city": "Seattle", "age": 31}
person.update(new_info)
```
If a key exists, its value gets updated. If it doesn't, Python adds it like a friendly intern. You can also merge with the | operator (Python 3.9+):

```python
CopyEdit
merged = dict1 | dict2
```
Merging has never felt so modern.

14.

Sometimes you want to create a dictionary from scratch—dynamically. Use `dict()` with keyword arguments:

```python
CopyEdit
car = dict(make="Subaru", model="Outback", year=2020)
```
Or from a list of tuples:

```python
CopyEdit
pairs = [("a", 1), ("b", 2)]
my_dict = dict(pairs)
```
There's also `fromkeys()` if you want all keys to share a default value. Python gives you many roads to Dictionaryville.

15.

Default values are handy with `.get()` or `setdefault()`.

```python
CopyEdit
person.get("nickname", "No nickname")
```
Or:

```python
CopyEdit
person.setdefault("nickname", "N/A")
```
The first *reads* safely, the second *adds* if missing. Great for when you're unsure whether a key exists. You can prevent crashes and provide smart fallbacks. Python believes in graceful degradation.

16.

Dictionaries are amazing for counting. Use them like tally charts:

```python
CopyEdit
votes = {}
for name in ["Alice", "Bob", "Alice"]:
    votes[name] = votes.get(name, 0) + 1
```
This tallies votes using `.get()` as a counter initializer. Want even more power? Use `collections.defaultdict`—it sets default values automatically. Python is surprisingly political.

17.

Dictionaries are also used in **JSON** data. JSON stands for JavaScript Object Notation—but

Python reads and writes it fluently. It's basically a dictionary with a fancy passport. Use the `json` module to load and dump data:

```python
CopyEdit
import json
data = json.loads('{"name": "Ada"}')
print(data["name"])
```

This is how APIs, configs, and data pipelines work behind the scenes. Python's dictionaries speak fluent Internet.

18.

Let's play with dictionary comprehension:

```python
CopyEdit
squares = {x: x**2 for x in range(5)}
```

This creates a dictionary where keys are numbers and values are their squares. You can filter too:

```python
CopyEdit
evens = {x: x**2 for x in range(10) if x % 2 == 0}
```

It's compact, expressive, and efficient. Dictionary comprehension is the espresso of data creation — strong and concise.

19.

Let's say you want to flip a dictionary — swap keys and values.

```python
CopyEdit
original = {"a": 1, "b": 2}
flipped = {v: k for k, v in original.items()}
```

Just make sure all values are unique and immutable. Python won't let you use lists as keys. Flipping gives you reverse lookups, inverted maps, and power tools for data transforms. Be careful — it's easy to lose data if values repeat.

20.

Your challenge: build a basic student gradebook. Let the user enter names and grades. Store them in a dictionary. Then print each student with their grade. Add a way to update a grade and remove a student. You now have a basic CRUD system (Create, Read, Update, Delete). Welcome to backend basics.

21.

Let's recap: dictionaries store data in key-value pairs. They're mutable, dynamic, and crazy useful. You can access, update, delete, and loop through them easily. They scale beautifully and adapt to almost any task. Whether you're building a user database or translating emoji to animal names, dictionaries have your back. They're the backbone of data in Python. And you've just unlocked another core superpower.

22.
Next up: **Tuples & Sets – The Low-Maintenance Siblings**. Tuples are lists that refuse to change. Sets are unordered collections that hate duplicates. You'll learn when to use each, how to harness their quirks, and why they're the unsung heroes of Python. But for now—enjoy your well-organized chaos. You're a dictionary master.

Chapter 9: Tuples & Sets – The Low-Maintenance Siblings

1.
After the dynamic drama of lists and the organizational obsession of dictionaries, it's time to meet Python's more relaxed relatives: **tuples** and **sets**. Think of them as the introverts of the data structure family. Tuples are like lists that don't want to be changed—once created, they're set in stone (or, technically, immutable). Sets, on the other hand, are like lists with commitment issues—they don't care about order, don't allow duplicates, and refuse to hold the same thing twice. Both are lean, efficient, and super useful in the right context. You won't always use them, but when you do, you'll be glad they're there. If lists are grocery bags, then tuples are sealed lunchboxes, and sets are minimalist pantries. Let's unpack them.

2.
Let's start with **tuples**. You create one by using parentheses instead of brackets:

```python
CopyEdit
coordinates = (10.0, 20.0)
```
That's a tuple with two floats. You can store any type—strings, numbers, even other tuples. But here's the deal: **you can't modify it**. Tuples are immutable, which means no appending, removing, or reassigning elements. They're ideal for data you want to protect—coordinates, config values, or anything labeled "DO NOT TOUCH."

3.
Tuples look deceptively like lists but act like stubborn goats. Try this:

```python
CopyEdit
t = (1, 2, 3)
t[0] = 99  # Error time!
```

You'll get a `TypeError` because Python won't let you change any part of it. That might sound limiting, but it's actually a **feature**, not a bug. Immutability makes tuples **faster** and **safer** than lists in many scenarios. If data shouldn't change, make it a tuple. Python takes that promise seriously.

4.
Want to create a one-item tuple? You need a comma.

```python
CopyEdit
solo = (42,)
```
Without the comma, it's just a number in parentheses—Python shrugs it off. The comma is what signals a tuple, not the parentheses. Weird? A little. But that's Python for you: elegant with a hint of quirk. Two-item tuples are easy, but the one-item club has an exclusive comma rule.

5.
You can access tuple elements using indexing, just like with lists.

```python
CopyEdit
t = ("red", "green", "blue")
print(t[1])   # green
```
Negative indexing works too: `t[-1]` is `"blue"`. You can slice them, loop through them, and unpack them like a polite Python gift box:

```python
CopyEdit
r, g, b = t
```
Tuple unpacking is slick and useful for assigning multiple variables at once. Think of it as Python's version of opening a three-part fortune cookie.

6.
Want to return multiple values from a function? Tuples to the rescue!

```python
CopyEdit
def get_position():
    return (10, 20)

x, y = get_position()
```
This is clean, readable, and immensely useful. Python silently wraps multiple return values in a tuple. The caller can then unpack it in one smooth move. It's like teleporting multiple data pieces in a single line. Tuples are the Swiss Army knives of return values.

7.

Tuples can be nested, combined, and even used as dictionary **keys**. That's right—because they're immutable, tuples can be hashed and used where lists can't.

```python
CopyEdit
data = {("NY", "LA"): 3000}
```
You can't do that with a list—Python would burst into flames. Tuples are safe, stable, and reliable. They play nicely with memory and won't randomly mutate behind your back. Great for when data integrity matters.

8.

Let's shift gears to **sets**—Python's answer to "Do we really need duplicates?" A set is an unordered collection of unique values. You create it with curly braces, just like a dictionary—but without colons.

```python
CopyEdit
colors = {"red", "green", "blue"}
```
No duplicates allowed. Order? Nope. Sets are like party guests that don't stay in their assigned seats, but at least they don't show up twice.

9.

Let's prove the uniqueness rule:

```python
CopyEdit
colors = {"red", "green", "red"}
print(colors)  # {'green', 'red'}
```
Only one `"red"` sticks around. Python silently discards duplicates like a no-nonsense bouncer. This is perfect for deduplicating lists:

```python
CopyEdit
unique_names = set(["Alice", "Bob", "Alice"])
```
Now `"Alice"` only appears once. Sets don't do drama.

10.

You can't access set items by index because sets are **unordered**.

```python
CopyEdit
colors[0]  # Nope! Raises TypeError.
```
Want to check membership? Use `in`:

```python
CopyEdit
"red" in colors
```
That's lightning-fast because sets are optimized for lookups. Think of them like Python's private search engine. Behind the scenes, they use hash tables. Translation: fast and efficient.

11.

To create an empty set, you **must** use `set()`.

```python
CopyEdit
empty = set()
```
Using `{}` creates an empty **dictionary**, not a set. This is one of those gotcha moments that trips up even seasoned coders. So remember: curly braces with items = set, but empty curly braces = dictionary. If you need an empty set, spell it out. Python appreciates the clarity.

12.

You can add and remove items with `.add()` and `.remove()`:

```python
CopyEdit
colors.add("yellow")
colors.remove("blue")
```
Trying to remove an item that doesn't exist causes a `KeyError`. Want to be safe?
Use `.discard()` instead—it removes the item if it exists and stays silent if it doesn't. There's also `.pop()`, but it removes a random item because sets have no order. Deleting at random—what could go wrong?

13.

Now let's talk set operations—this is where sets shine.

- **Union (|)** combines sets.

- **Intersection (&)** finds common items.

- **Difference (−)** removes items from one set that exist in another.

- **Symmetric difference (^)** returns items not in both.
  Example:

```python
CopyEdit
a = {1, 2, 3}
b = {3, 4, 5}
print(a | b)  # {1, 2, 3, 4, 5}
```

Set math is beautiful chaos.

14.

You can also use methods like `.union()`, `.intersection()`, and `.difference()` —more readable but a tad longer.

```python
CopyEdit
a.union(b)
a.intersection(b)
a.difference(b)
```

Same results, same logic. Use the version that makes your code easier to read. Operators are great for short scripts. Methods are clearer in longer code. Both are equally valid—Python lets you pick your flavor.

15.

Sets are great for filtering duplicates:

```python
CopyEdit
nums = [1, 2, 2, 3, 4, 4]
unique = list(set(nums))
```

This is a one-liner magic trick. Toss the list into a set to strip duplicates, then convert it back. Clean, fast, and surprisingly satisfying. Your dataset now sparkles with uniqueness.

16.

You can loop through sets just like lists:

```python
CopyEdit
for color in colors:
    print(color)
```

The only caveat: order isn't guaranteed. So don't depend on print order unless you enjoy mild confusion. Sets are like grabbing handfuls of Skittles—you'll get them all, but never in the order you expect.

17.

Set comparisons are a thing:

- `subset = a <= b` checks if `a` is a subset of `b`.

- `superset = a >= b` checks if `a` contains all elements of `b`.

- `a == b` checks if they're equal.

- a != b confirms they're not.
  These work great for permissions, tags, or access control. Python gives you the logical tools. You bring the rules.

18.

Frozensets exist too—they're immutable sets.

```python
CopyEdit
frozen = frozenset([1, 2, 3])
```

They support all the set operations, but you can't add or remove items. Useful when you want set behavior without the danger of change. And yes, they can be dictionary keys or stored in other sets. Immutability strikes again!

19.

Tuples and sets aren't flashy, but they're powerful in the right hands. Tuples bring reliability and fixed structure. Sets bring speed and duplicate resistance. When combined with lists and dictionaries, they complete your data structure toolkit. Think of them as tools for **intent**. When you use a tuple, you're saying, "This won't change." When you use a set, you're saying, "I only care about what's here, not how it's ordered."

20.

Here's your challenge:

- Create a list with duplicate entries.

- Convert it into a set to remove duplicates.

- Turn it back into a list.

- Then group related items into a tuple and store them in a dictionary.
  You just used all four major data structures—and looked cool doing it. Python high-five!

21.

Let's review. Tuples are immutable, indexable, and great for stable data. Sets are unordered, unindexed, and perfect for membership tests and unique collections. Both bring safety and clarity to your code. They won't be your everyday tools, but they'll absolutely be your favorite **situational** ones. When used right, they simplify logic and boost performance. You now know when and how to reach for them. Python's calmest siblings are officially in your toolkit.

22.

Next up: **Functions – Reusable Logic That Makes You Look Smart**. You'll learn how to write your own blocks of code, pass in parameters, and return meaningful results. Functions are the brain cells of programming—and it's time to grow a few. You've wrangled variables, tamed data structures, and now... it's time to write code that *thinks*.

Chapter 10: Functions – Reusable Logic That Makes You Look Smart

1.

Congratulations—you've reached the chapter where your code gets **brains**. If variables are your data and loops are your rhythm, then functions are your **thought process**. A function is like a mini-program inside your program—a reusable block of code you can call again and again without retyping. It's Python's way of saying, "Let's work smarter, not harder." Functions reduce repetition, increase clarity, and make you look like a programming genius. Instead of writing the same logic 12 times, you wrap it in a function and reuse it like a champion. Even the Python gods use functions—it's how the language works under the hood. So let's lift the curtain and see how it's done.

2.

The basic structure of a function starts with the `def` keyword.

```python
CopyEdit
def greet():
    print("Hello!")
```

You've just created your first function! To run it, simply call it: `greet()`. Python will execute everything indented under the function definition. No indent? No function. The parentheses are essential—they tell Python, "I mean business."

3.

Functions get a lot more interesting when you give them **parameters**.

```python
CopyEdit
def greet(name):
    print(f"Hello, {name}!")
```

Now it's a personalized greeting machine. Call it like this: `greet("Alice")`. Parameters are placeholders for input—temporary names for values the function expects. They make your functions adaptable and customizable. It's like writing your own fill-in-the-blank logic.

4.

Want to handle **multiple** inputs? Easy.

```python
CopyEdit
def add(a, b):
    return a + b
```

Here, a and b are parameters, and the function **returns** a value using the `return` keyword. This is different from `print()`—return actually hands data *back* to the caller. You can store it in a variable:

```python
CopyEdit
sum = add(5, 3)
```

Now your function is both smart and productive.

5.

Let's talk about `return`. Every function returns **something**—even if it's just `None`.

```python
CopyEdit
def nothing():
    pass
```

Calling `nothing()` returns `None` by default. So always think about what your function gives back. If it doesn't return a value, it's still useful (like printing or logging), but you won't be able to reuse its result. `return` is Python's way of saying, "Here you go—use this however you like."

6.

You can return **multiple values** using a tuple:

```python
CopyEdit
def get_stats():
    return 100, 200
x, y = get_stats()
```

Behind the scenes, Python packs those values into a tuple. It's simple, elegant, and oh-so-readable. You can use tuple unpacking to assign values on the fly. Returning multiple things is a superpower—and Python makes it painless. Use it wisely.

7.

You can also set **default values** for parameters.

```python
CopyEdit
def greet(name="Friend"):
    print(f"Hello, {name}!")
```

If you call `greet()` with no argument, it defaults to `"Friend"`. But call `greet("Bob")` and it uses your input. Defaults make functions flexible and forgiving. They're perfect for optional behavior and backward compatibility.

8.

Need more flexibility? Use `*args` and `**kwargs`.

```python
CopyEdit
def print_args(*args):
    for arg in args:
        print(arg)
```

`*args` collects all **positional** arguments into a tuple. `**kwargs` collects **keyword** arguments into a dictionary. Together, they make your function capable of handling any combination of inputs. It's Python's way of saying, "Bring it on."

9.

Here's a keyword argument example:

```python
CopyEdit
def show_info(**kwargs):
    for key, value in kwargs.items():
        print(f"{key}: {value}")
```

Call it like this: `show_info(name="Alice", age=30)`. You'll get labeled output without needing to define every possible parameter in advance. Great for config files, options, or API-like flexibility. Your function becomes a chameleon.

10.

Functions can call other functions. This is how complex programs are built—small pieces that talk to each other. It's like assembling a robot out of robot parts. Each function handles one job, then passes its result to the next. Keep functions focused—don't let one try to do *everything*. That's how you get spaghetti code and tears. Clear, single-purpose functions are the backbone of maintainable code.

11.

Let's talk **scope**. Variables created inside a function live **only** inside that function. This is called **local scope**.

```python
CopyEdit
def demo():
    x = 10
```

Try printing `x` outside the function, and Python will throw a fit. Variables declared outside are **global**—they live across the whole program. Scope keeps your logic compartmentalized and safe. Don't be surprised when your carefully crafted `score` inside a function vanishes outside it.

12.

Global variables can be accessed inside functions, but modifying them requires a keyword:

```python
CopyEdit
count = 0
def increment():
    global count
    count += 1
```

Use `global` carefully—shared state can create bugs if not managed well. Better approach? Return values instead. Global variables are like public bathrooms—use only when necessary.

13.

Python supports **docstrings**—in-function documentation.

```python
CopyEdit
def greet():
    """Prints a friendly greeting."""
    print("Hi!")
```

This isn't just for show—docstrings are accessible via `help(greet)` or `greet.__doc__`. Write them to explain what your function does, its parameters, and return value. It's a love letter to future you—or your coworkers. Documenting is coding with compassion.

14.

Lambda functions are anonymous, one-liner functions.

```python
CopyEdit
square = lambda x: x * x
print(square(5))
```

They're compact and great for short, throwaway logic—especially in filters, maps, or GUI callbacks. But don't go overboard. If it needs more than one line, use a regular function. Lambdas are clever but not meant for novels.

15.

Functions can be passed **as arguments**—yes, functions are **first-class citizens** in Python.

```python
CopyEdit
def shout(text):
    return text.upper()
def whisper(text):
```

```python
    return text.lower()
def speak(func, msg):
    print(func(msg))
speak(shout, "hello")
```

You just passed logic into logic. This opens the door to higher-order functions and fancy behaviors.

16.
Functions can also be **returned** from other functions.

python
CopyEdit
```python
def outer():
    def inner():
        return "Hello from inner!"
    return inner
f = outer()
print(f())
```

This is how decorators and function factories work. It sounds complex, but it's just nesting. Python doesn't care how many layers deep you go—it always knows where the parentheses end.

17.
Want to run a function conditionally? Just store it in a variable.

python
CopyEdit
```python
actions = {"greet": greet, "shout": shout}
actions["shout"]("python!")
```

This lets you create command maps, menus, or plugin systems. When functions are just data, your code becomes dynamic. It's Python at its most flexible—and it makes you look smart.

18.
Functions aren't just for reuse—they're for **organization**. Splitting your logic into named blocks makes it readable, testable, and less overwhelming. Imagine scrolling through 500 lines of unstructured code. Now imagine neatly labeled sections, each handling a specific job. Functions are the bookmarks of your logic. Use them liberally. Future-you will send flowers.

19.
Need to test your function? Call it with different inputs. Try edge cases—empty strings, zero, None, large values. Print the results or use `assert` to validate expectations.

python
CopyEdit
```python
assert add(2, 2) == 4
```

Testing helps you catch bugs early and code with confidence. A function that works right every time? That's power.

20.
Here's your mini challenge:

- Write a function to convert Fahrenheit to Celsius.

- Add a docstring.

- Handle default input if none is provided.

- Call it with a few test values.
  You've just created a utility function—something real programs use all the time. Small, smart, and infinitely reusable.

21.
Let's recap. Functions are blocks of reusable logic that take input, process it, and (usually) return output. They reduce repetition, organize code, and open the door to more advanced techniques like lambdas, callbacks, and decorators. You've learned how to define, call, nest, return, and even pass them around like hot potatoes. Functions are where your code starts to **think**. They're the gears in your logic machine. And now—you're the engineer.

22.
Next up: **Modules & Libraries – Calling in the Reinforcements**. Because why reinvent the wheel when Python has a whole garage of them? We'll explore built-in tools, how to import them, and even how to write your own. The function train continues—this time with **packs of prewritten power**. Let's level up your toolbox.

Chapter 11: Modules & Libraries – Calling in the Reinforcements

1.
At some point, every Python programmer asks themselves, "Wait, surely someone has written this already?" Good news—they have. In fact, entire legions of Pythonistas have been writing useful code and packaging it up into beautiful, reusable **modules** and **libraries**. You don't have to build a calculator, JSON parser, or data visualizer from scratch—Python's ecosystem has your back. Modules are individual files of Python code; libraries are collections of modules, often bundled with related tools. Together, they form Python's most powerful advantage: **code reuse at superhero scale**. You're not just coding anymore—you're **assembling an army**. All you need is `import`.

2.

Let's start small. Python ships with a huge collection of modules called the **standard library**. These include everything from date handling to file management, math to networking. You access them with a simple keyword:

```python
CopyEdit
import math
print(math.sqrt(16))  # 4.0
```

Boom—you just unlocked square roots with one line. No need to write the function yourself. That's Python's standard library saving you time and brain cells.

3.

Want to only import part of a module? Use `from`:

```python
CopyEdit
from math import pi
print(pi)  # 3.14159...
```

This brings `pi` directly into your program, no `math.` prefix required. It's great for keeping things short and sweet. You can even rename imports with `as`:

```python
CopyEdit
import math as m
print(m.sqrt(25))
```

Now your imports are both efficient and stylish.

4.

Let's check out the `random` module—it's fun, friendly, and perfect for chaos.

```python
CopyEdit
import random
print(random.randint(1, 10))
```

This gives you a random integer between 1 and 10. Want to shuffle a list? Use `random.shuffle(my_list)`. Want to simulate a coin flip? `random.choice(["heads", "tails"])`. With `random`, your code gains unpredictability—which is exactly what games, simulations, and Friday afternoons need.

5.

Need to work with **dates and times**? Python's got `datetime`:

```python
```

```
from datetime import datetime
now = datetime.now()
print(now)
```

You can format it, extract components, or do date math.

python

```
print(now.year, now.month, now.day)
```

There's also `timedelta` for durations—add or subtract time like a time-traveling wizard. Python makes calendars feel cool.

6.

Dealing with files? Meet `os` and `pathlib`.

python

```
import os
print(os.getcwd())  # Get current directory
```

`os` is great for environment variables and system paths. `pathlib` is more modern and object-oriented:

python

```
from pathlib import Path
print(Path.cwd())
```

It's the new school way to navigate files, folders, and the occasional existential crisis caused by long paths.

7.

Let's talk about `sys`—Python's backstage pass.

python

```
import sys
print(sys.version)
```

You can access command-line arguments, system paths, and the Python runtime. Want to exit a script? `sys.exit()`. Want to access script arguments? `sys.argv`. `sys` is like Python's remote control—use it wisely.

8.

Python has a module for just about everything. Need regular expressions? `import re`. Need internet access? Try `urllib` or `requests`. Want to handle JSON?

```python
CopyEdit
import json
data = '{"name": "Ada", "age": 30}'
parsed = json.loads(data)
print(parsed["name"])
```
Python speaks many data dialects. You just need to ask.

9.

The standard library is powerful, but sometimes you need **third-party reinforcements**. Enter the **Python Package Index (PyPI)**—a global buffet of libraries written by generous developers. You install these packages using `pip`, Python's package installer:

```bash
CopyEdit
pip install requests
```
Once installed, you can import it like any other module. Thousands of libraries await—data science, web dev, automation, AI, and beyond.

10.

Let's talk about the beloved `requests` library.

```python
CopyEdit
import requests
response = requests.get("https://api.github.com")
print(response.status_code)
```
Now your Python script can **talk to the internet**. Fetch data, call APIs, even send forms. With just a few lines, you've turned your code into a web-aware entity. That's how modern apps get their news.

11.

Need data wrangling power? `pandas` is your go-to.

```python
CopyEdit
import pandas as pd
data = pd.read_csv("data.csv")
```
Now you've loaded a spreadsheet into Python. Sort it, filter it, analyze it—`pandas` gives you spreadsheet superpowers. It's popular for data science, automation, and impressing your manager with colorful charts.

12.

For number crunching, say hello to `numpy`:

```python
CopyEdit
import numpy as np
a = np.array([1, 2, 3])
print(a * 2)   # [2, 4, 6]
```
You just did vectorized math—no loops required. numpy is the bedrock of scientific computing. It's also really fast, thanks to C-level performance behind the scenes.

13.
Want to visualize data? Bring in matplotlib:

```python
CopyEdit
import matplotlib.pyplot as plt
plt.plot([1, 2, 3], [4, 1, 9])
plt.show()
```
You've just drawn your first chart. Visualization turns numbers into stories. And Python's libraries make it beautiful—even if your design skills peaked with stick figures.

14.
Need automation? Try pyautogui:

```python
CopyEdit
import pyautogui
pyautogui.moveTo(100, 100, duration=1)
```
Now your script controls your mouse—yes, really. You can write bots, automate UI tests, or mess with your coworkers (ethically, of course). Python isn't just brainy—it can *move*.

15.
Want to build a web app? Try flask:

```python
CopyEdit
from flask import Flask
app = Flask(__name__)

@app.route("/")
def home():
    return "Hello from Flask!"
```
You just built a web server in five lines. Flask is lightweight, fun, and easy to learn. It's like Django's chill cousin.

16.

Sometimes you'll want to **create your own module**. Just write a `.py` file and import it elsewhere.

```python
# helpers.py
def greet(name):
    return f"Hello, {name}!"
```

Then in another file:

```python
import helpers
print(helpers.greet("Ada"))
```

Boom—code reuse made personal. This is how big apps stay organized.

17.

If you create a lot of files, consider using **packages**—folders with `__init__.py`. This signals to Python: "This folder contains modules." You can organize by topic, version, or pure vibes. Packages keep your code scalable and sane. Especially when you're building something larger than a to-do list.

18.

Want to know what modules are available in your environment? Use `help("modules")` in the interpreter. Or check installed packages:

```bash
pip list
```

You'll see a glorious list of what's available. Just don't try to import `antigravity`—unless you want a very Pythonic Easter egg.

19.

To upgrade or uninstall a package, use pip again:

```bash
pip install --upgrade requests
pip uninstall pandas
```

Package management is smooth—just be mindful of dependencies. Use a **virtual environment** (`venv`) to isolate your projects. That way, one upgrade doesn't break twelve other things.

20.

Here's your challenge:

- Pick a PyPI library (like `requests` or `pyfiglet`)

- Install it with pip

- Write a small script that uses it
  You just joined the ranks of thousands of real-world Python developers. Working with libraries is how Python scales from small scripts to billion-dollar applications.

21.

Let's recap. Modules are files of reusable code. The standard library gives you a strong foundation. Third-party libraries supercharge your projects. Pip installs them, and `import` unlocks them. You don't have to do it all yourself. Python's community already did the heavy lifting. You just need to know where to look.

22.

Next up: **File Handling – Read, Write, and Rock 'n' Roll**. You'll learn how to open, read, write, and manage files with style. We're talking about everything from reading log files to writing your own. Ready to make your programs interact with the outside world? Let's go grab some files.

Chapter 12: File Handling – Read, Write, and Rock 'n' Roll

1.

Welcome to the chapter where Python meets the **real world**—and by that, we mean files. Files are how we store data outside the fleeting memory of a program. Whether you're reading a config file, writing a user log, or exporting JSON like a pro, file handling is a skill you can't skip. Python makes it surprisingly painless—no digital blood sacrifices required. You'll learn how to open, read, write, and manipulate files like a rock star. Think of it as stage-managing your own data concert. You're about to learn how to load the lyrics and save the encore. Let's open that file like it's a backstage pass.

2.

The first rule of file handling: use the `open()` function.

```python
CopyEdit
file = open("notes.txt", "r")
```

This line tells Python to open `notes.txt` in **read** mode. Modes matter—`"r"` is for reading, `"w"` is for writing (overwrite), `"a"` is for appending, and `"x"` is for exclusive creation. Want to read a file's content?

python

```python
content = file.read()
print(content)
```

Just don't forget to close the file when you're done—Python's polite like that.

3.

Seriously—close your files!

python

```python
file.close()
```

Not doing so can lead to memory leaks or file locks, especially in larger applications. But instead of manually closing every time, use a `with` block:

python

```python
with open("notes.txt", "r") as file:
    content = file.read()
```

This ensures the file is automatically closed—even if your script crashes mid-song. It's safer, cleaner, and more Pythonic. Your future self will thank you.

4.

Let's talk modes.

- `"r"`: read-only

- `"w"`: write (overwrites existing)

- `"a"`: append

- `"x"`: exclusive creation (fails if file exists)

- `"r+"`: read and write
  When in doubt, `"r"` is the safe starting point. `"w"` will erase everything in the file—so be careful not to turn your tax report into blank space. Always choose your mode like you're choosing a difficulty level in a game.

5.

Reading a file all at once? Use `.read()`.

python

```python
with open("data.txt", "r") as file:
    content = file.read()
```

This returns the entire file as one long string. Need just a single line? Use `.readline()`. Want all lines in a list? Try `.readlines()`—each line becomes a list item. These methods give you flexible control. Pick your read style based on your appetite.

6.

Let's loop through a file line by line:

```python
CopyEdit
with open("data.txt", "r") as file:
    for line in file:
        print(line.strip())
```

This is memory-efficient and easy to read. `strip()` removes that pesky newline character at the end. This method is perfect for logs, large files, or streaming text. Looping through a file is like reading a script—line by line, no spoilers. You're now the narrator of your own data.

7.

Now, onto **writing**.

```python
CopyEdit
with open("output.txt", "w") as file:
    file.write("Hello, world!")
```

This creates the file if it doesn't exist, and **overwrites** it if it does. If you want to add without deleting, use `"a"` for append mode. Each `write()` call puts data in without a newline—add `\n` if you want line breaks. You're now officially a file author. Time to publish something useful (or at least hilarious).

8.

Want to write multiple lines? Pass a list to `writelines()`:

```python
CopyEdit
lines = ["First line\n", "Second line\n"]
file.writelines(lines)
```

But remember—`writelines()` does not automatically add line breaks. So either include `\n` manually or loop through the list and call `write()` line by line. It's one of those Python quirks that keeps you humble. The good news? Once you master it, you can write to any text file like a wizard.

9.

Need to **check** if a file exists? Python's got your back:

```python
CopyEdit
```

```
import os
if os.path.exists("data.txt"):
    print("File found!")
```
This is especially helpful before writing, deleting, or opening a file in `"x"` mode. You can also check if it's a file or directory:

python
CopyEdit
```
os.path.isfile("data.txt")
os.path.isdir("my_folder")
```
No more guessing—or accidentally writing over your resume.

10.
Let's get fancy with **file paths**. Use raw strings or double backslashes on Windows:

python
CopyEdit
```
open("C:\\Users\\YourName\\file.txt", "r")
# or
open(r"C:\Users\YourName\file.txt", "r")
```
Better yet, use `pathlib`:

python
CopyEdit
```
from pathlib import Path
file = Path("data.txt")
```
It works across platforms and gives you cleaner path manipulation. You'll thank yourself when your script works on Linux, Windows, and macOS without changes.

11.
Let's talk **file deletion**.

python
CopyEdit
```
os.remove("old_file.txt")
```
Simple, effective, permanent. Always check that the file exists first—or wrap in a `try/ except` block to catch errors gracefully. Deleting files with Python should feel powerful—but also a little terrifying. With great power comes great `FileNotFoundError` handling.

12.
Want to create or rename directories? Use `os.mkdir()` and `os.rename()`:

python
CopyEdit

```python
os.mkdir("new_folder")
os.rename("old.txt", "renamed.txt")
```
Or go full Zen with `pathlib` again:

```python
CopyEdit
Path("cool_folder").mkdir(exist_ok=True)
```
You're now managing your own file empire. Call it Filetopia.

13.

Let's read and write **CSV files**—a favorite of spreadsheets everywhere.

```python
CopyEdit
import csv
with open("scores.csv", "w", newline="") as file:
    writer = csv.writer(file)
    writer.writerow(["Name", "Score"])
    writer.writerow(["Alice", 95])
```
Want to read it?

```python
CopyEdit
with open("scores.csv", "r") as file:
    reader = csv.reader(file)
    for row in reader:
        print(row)
```
Welcome to structured data. No Excel required.

14.

How about **JSON**? Python makes it smooth:

```python
CopyEdit
import json
data = {"name": "Ada", "age": 30}
with open("user.json", "w") as file:
    json.dump(data, file)
```
To load:

```python
CopyEdit
with open("user.json", "r") as file:
    user = json.load(file)
```

Great for APIs, settings, or passing data between programs. JSON is like dictionaries—only slightly more fashionable.

15.

Want to store raw binary files like images or executables? Use binary mode:

- `"rb"` = read binary

- `"wb"` = write binary
  This is how you copy or save non-text files:

```python
CopyEdit
with open("image.jpg", "rb") as source:
    data = source.read()
with open("copy.jpg", "wb") as target:
    target.write(data)
```

Python isn't just for text—it plays in every data format band.

16.

Now let's talk safety. Always use `try/except` when handling files:

```python
CopyEdit
try:
    with open("secret.txt") as f:
        content = f.read()
except FileNotFoundError:
    print("File not found!")
```

This prevents crashes and shows you care. Error handling is the difference between a script and a solution.

17.

File input/output (I/O) isn't just about storage—it's about communication. Your programs can read logs, export reports, or automate tasks across hundreds of files. File handling gives you permanence. It lets your code speak across time. You're no longer printing to the void—you're creating a written legacy. (Even if it's just a list of dad jokes.)

18.

Want to process multiple files in a folder?

```python
CopyEdit
for file in os.listdir("my_folder"):
    if file.endswith(".txt"):
```

```
        print(file)
```
You just built a mini search engine. Combine this with open(), read(), and boom—you're analyzing an entire directory like a digital archaeologist. Python turns your filesystem into a playground.

19.
Your mini challenge:

- Ask the user for their name and favorite color

- Save that data to a text file

- Reopen the file and display the content
  Bonus: timestamp the entry and append to the file instead of overwriting. Boom—your first logging system. It's not just a script. It's a journal.

20.
Let's review. File handling means opening, reading, writing, and managing files and folders. Python supports text, CSV, JSON, and binary formats. Use `with open()` to stay clean. Use `os` and `pathlib` to move around like a pro. Always handle errors with grace. And never underestimate the power of the filesystem.

21.
By now, you've learned how to save and share your program's thoughts. File handling opens doors—storing user data, exporting results, importing templates, and more. Python doesn't just *think* anymore. It remembers. And that, my friend, is how programs level up.

22.
Next up: **Error Handling – Code Without Crashing and Crying**. Because things will go wrong. Files will vanish. Data will misbehave. And you'll learn to catch those moments like a pro. Grab your safety goggles—it's time to tame the exceptions.

Chapter 13: Error Handling – Try, Except, Breathe

1.
Let's face it—things go wrong. Files go missing, users type in emojis instead of numbers, and programs crash harder than your Wi-Fi at 2 AM. But you, brave coder, are about to learn **how to fail with style**. Python gives us tools to detect errors, catch them mid-air, and even recover gracefully. This magical process is called **exception handling**, and it starts with two simple words: `try` and `except`. You're about to build a safety net for your code—a digital parachute.

With it, you can prevent crashes, protect data, and keep your users (and boss) from rage-quitting. Deep breath. Try. Except. Breathe.

2.

So, what's an **exception**? It's Python's way of saying, "I don't know what you want from me right now." It's not necessarily your fault—it could be a missing file, a divide-by-zero, or a user entering "banana" instead of an integer. When Python encounters an error it can't handle, it **raises** an exception. If you don't catch it, your script halts, flashes red, and dumps a lovely traceback all over your screen. But with a `try` block, you can **catch** the exception and keep going like a pro. It's the difference between face-planting and doing a graceful somersault.

3.

Here's a basic structure:

```python
CopyEdit
try:
    risky_code()
except:
    print("Something went wrong.")
```

Everything inside the `try` block is attempted. If something explodes, Python jumps into the `except` block and lets you handle it. This prevents the crash and gives you control over how to respond. No panic. No drama. Just cool, calm code.

4.

You can catch specific error types.

```python
CopyEdit
try:
    1 / 0
except ZeroDivisionError:
    print("Can't divide by zero!")
```

This lets you tailor your error response. Different exceptions mean different problems. You wouldn't respond to a `FileNotFoundError` the same way you would a `ValueError`. Be precise—it's better than a vague "Oops!" message. Python's exceptions are named, categorized, and ready to be handled.

5.

Common exception types include:

- `ZeroDivisionError`: dividing by zero

- `ValueError`: invalid data type (like turning `"abc"` into an `int`)

- `TypeError`: using the wrong type in an operation

- `FileNotFoundError`: trying to open a file that doesn't exist

- `IndexError`: accessing an index that's out of bounds
  Each of these can be caught specifically. Think of them as different kinds of fire. You don't use the same extinguisher on electrical and grease fires—why do that in code?

6.

Want to handle multiple exceptions? Stack them like pancakes:

python
CopyEdit
```python
try:
    risky_business()
except FileNotFoundError:
    print("File not found.")
except ValueError:
    print("Bad input.")
```
Python checks them in order, top to bottom. If none match, the error still escapes like a rogue raccoon. Always catch the most specific ones first. It's like putting out the small sparks before the big blaze.

7.

You can also catch **everything** with a generic `except` block—*but be careful.*

python
CopyEdit
```python
try:
    mystery_code()
except Exception as e:
    print(f"Error: {e}")
```
This is helpful in quick scripts or when debugging something unpredictable. But overusing it hides problems and makes bugs harder to find. If your code silently swallows exceptions, you might miss critical failures. Use it sparingly, like hot sauce.

8.

Let's talk about the **else** block.

python
CopyEdit
```python
try:
    result = 10 / 2
except ZeroDivisionError:
```

```python
        print("You divided by zero.")
else:
        print("Everything went fine!")
```

The `else` block runs **only if no exceptions occur**. It's a great way to separate success logic from failure logic. It keeps your code clean and makes your intent crystal clear. If it runs, it means the `try` was smooth as jazz.

9.

Then there's the **`finally`** block—the cleanup crew.

python
CopyEdit
```python
try:
        file = open("data.txt")
except FileNotFoundError:
        print("Missing file.")
finally:
        print("This runs no matter what.")
```

`finally` always executes, no matter what happened above. Perfect for closing files, releasing resources, or sending an "I'm still alive" message. Even if you `return` or raise another error, the `finally` block gets the last word.

10.

You can **raise** your own exceptions with the `raise` keyword:

python
CopyEdit
```python
if age < 0:
        raise ValueError("Age can't be negative!")
```

This is useful when something goes wrong that Python wouldn't automatically detect. You're taking charge of the chaos. Custom exceptions can make your code more predictable and easier to debug. You're not just reacting to errors—you're calling them out.

11.

Want to make your own **custom exception class**? You fancy now.

python
CopyEdit
```python
class MyError(Exception):
        pass
raise MyError("Something custom went wrong.")
```

This lets you define exceptions with unique names and behaviors. You can even add extra data or methods. It's a little extra effort—but big apps love this level of control. You're no longer using exceptions. You're designing them.

12.

You can even **re-raise** exceptions:

```python
CopyEdit
try:
    something_dangerous()
except Exception as e:
    print("Logging the error...")
    raise
```

This logs the issue but still lets it bubble up. It's like saying, "I've seen it, I've noted it, but I'm not fixing it here." Useful for debugging or letting higher-level code take responsibility. Exceptions don't always have to be resolved immediately.

13.

Error messages are your friends. Don't just say "error happened"—be specific:

```python
CopyEdit
except ValueError as e:
    print(f"Invalid input: {e}")
```

Include what went wrong, where it happened, and what the user can do next. A good error message is like a GPS rerouting—annoying, but incredibly helpful. Don't leave people stranded. Even code deserves a soft landing.

14.

Exceptions aren't always bugs. Sometimes they're part of your app's logic. For example, if a user enters an invalid password, that's not a bug—it's a handled exception. Your job isn't just to fix things when they break. It's to **expect** them to break and handle it with grace. This mindset turns spaghetti code into Michelin-worthy logic.

15.

Let's say you're building a calculator. You'll want to catch:

- `ZeroDivisionError` (dividing by zero)

- `ValueError` (bad input)

- `TypeError` (invalid operations)
  Handle each with a user-friendly message. Let the app continue running. The best programs don't crash—they adapt. Be the duct tape of software.

16.

Errors can also be **logged** instead of just printed.

```python
CopyEdit
import logging
logging.error("Something failed", exc_info=True)
```
This keeps a record of problems without disrupting the user. Perfect for servers, tools, or anything running unsupervised. Logs give you visibility into what went wrong, when, and why. It's like a black box for your program—minus the crash.

17.

You don't need to catch **every** exception. Sometimes letting it crash is the right move. Especially in early development—it's better to see the problem clearly. Just make sure you're logging, documenting, or debugging wisely. Not every bug deserves a band-aid. But every crash deserves a cause.

18.

Your challenge:

- Ask the user for a number

- Try to divide 100 by that number

- Catch `ZeroDivisionError` and `ValueError`

- Print the result, or a friendly message if things go south
  You now have a resilient script. One that adjusts instead of imploding.

19.

Let's recap. Errors happen. But with `try`, `except`, `else`, and `finally`, you can respond with calm and clarity. Raise your own exceptions, catch the right ones, and write messages that help—not hinder. This is how software goes from "Oops" to "Handled." And you've got the skills now.

20.

Error handling isn't just about preventing crashes—it's about building **trust**. Users trust your app won't explode when they mistype. Devs trust your modules won't return `None` silently. Error handling is quiet excellence. Like a bodyguard in a tux. You know it's there—but you rarely see it unless things go wrong.

21.

You've now unlocked the ability to let your programs make mistakes—**without becoming one**. From file fails to divide-by-zero disasters, you're equipped to handle it all. And the best part? The more you practice error handling, the less terrifying bugs become. You become the calm in the chaos. The try in the exception storm.

Next up: **Object-Oriented Programming – Thinking in Classes and Objects**. Because Python isn't just procedural—it's also about **designing** your own data types. You'll learn how to bundle data and behavior into classes, create methods, and give your code a personality. Get ready to meet your inner architect.

Chapter 14: Object-Oriented Python – Classes Without the Homework

1.

Let's face it—the phrase "Object-Oriented Programming" (OOP) sounds like something your CS professor made up to scare you. But relax—it's not an algebraic cult. OOP is just a way to organize your code by bundling **data** (attributes) and **functions** (methods) into reusable blueprints called **classes**. It's like building custom Lego bricks—once you define the shape, you can build as many objects as you want. Python is fully OOP-capable, and it's incredibly beginner-friendly. Even if you've never "thought in classes," Python makes it easy. In this chapter, we'll demystify classes, objects, and methods—and maybe even have a little fun. Let's create code that not only works—but knows who it is.

2.

The heart of OOP is the **class**—a blueprint for creating objects.

```python
CopyEdit
class Dog:
    pass
```
This does absolutely nothing—but it's technically a class. A class defines **what something is**, and the objects created from it are called **instances**. Think of a class as a cookie cutter, and each object as a cookie. Same shape, unique dough. Now, let's teach our dog class to bark.

3.

Let's give it a method:

```python
CopyEdit
class Dog:
    def bark(self):
        print("Woof!")
```
Now we can **instantiate** (create) a dog and make it speak:

```python
CopyEdit
fido = Dog()
fido.bark()
```
Congratulations, you've created your first object and made it bark on command. You're officially a Python dog whisperer.

4.

What's that `self` thing? It's Python's way of saying "this object." Every method inside a class must take `self` as the first parameter—so it knows which instance it's talking to. It's not a keyword—it's just a strong tradition (don't rename it unless you like chaos). Think of `self` as the actor saying their own name on stage. It gives access to the object's own data and other methods. Without `self`, methods have **no idea** who they're working for. Poor, confused methods.

5.

Let's give our dog a **name** with an **initializer** method:

```python
CopyEdit
class Dog:
    def __init__(self, name):
        self.name = name
```
The `__init__` method is a **constructor**—it runs **automatically** when you create a new object. Now each dog has its own identity:

```python
CopyEdit
buddy = Dog("Buddy")
print(buddy.name)   # Buddy
```
Every time you call `Dog("X")`, it builds a new dog with a unique name. That's class in action.

6.

Let's add more personality:

```python
CopyEdit
class Dog:
    def __init__(self, name, breed):
        self.name = name
        self.breed = breed

    def bark(self):
        print(f"{self.name} the {self.breed} says: Woof!")
```

Now each object has multiple **attributes** (name, breed) and a method that uses them. It's like giving your data an identity **and** a voice. Your objects now walk and talk—digitally, of course.

7.

You can have **many objects** from the same class:

python
CopyEdit
```python
a = Dog("Max", "Labrador")
b = Dog("Luna", "Poodle")
```
They share the class blueprint but hold their own data. Each object is unique—like twins with different hobbies. You can interact with them independently:

python
CopyEdit
```python
a.bark()
b.bark()
```
This is the beauty of OOP—you build once, reuse infinitely.

8.

You can also **change attributes** after creation:

python
CopyEdit
```python
a.name = "Maximus"
print(a.name)
```
But be careful—you're modifying live objects. Always know what your code is touching. If you want to **lock in** attributes, make them private or read-only. Python doesn't enforce strict privacy, but it encourages good manners. We'll cover that shortly.

9.

Let's make a method that changes the dog's mood:

python
CopyEdit
```python
class Dog:
    def __init__(self, name):
        self.name = name
        self.happy = True

    def scold(self):
        self.happy = False
        print(f"{self.name} looks sad.")
```

```python
def treat(self):
    self.happy = True
    print(f"{self.name} wags its tail.")
```
Now you're storing **state** inside the object. Each method changes the object's internal world.

10.

Let's use `__str__()` to make our object print nicely:

```python
CopyEdit
def __str__(self):
    return f"{self.name} the Dog"
```
Now when you `print(dog)`, you don't get a weird memory address—you get a friendly name. It's like customizing your object's nametag. This is one of many **dunder** methods (double underscores) you can override. Python lets your objects behave like built-ins, if you give them the right tricks.

11.

Let's create a **Cat** class to compare:

```python
CopyEdit
class Cat:
    def __init__(self, name):
        self.name = name

    def meow(self):
        print(f"{self.name} says: Meow!")
```
Different class, different behavior. Now you can create cats and dogs that coexist in your digital zoo. They have nothing in common (yet), but they live by the same OOP rules. Classes are how you organize logic by **concept**, not just data.

12.

Ready to take it up a notch? Meet **inheritance**.

```python
CopyEdit
class Animal:
    def __init__(self, name):
        self.name = name

    def speak(self):
        print(f"{self.name} makes a sound.")
```
Now a dog can **inherit** from animal:

```python
CopyEdit
class Dog(Animal):
    def speak(self):
        print(f"{self.name} says: Woof!")
```
Inheritance lets you reuse and extend code without rewriting it. You're not copying—you're evolving.

13.

Inheritance supports **method overriding**—like when Dog redefined `speak()`. The child class (Dog) can override any method from the parent (Animal). If you still want to use the parent method, call it with `super()`:

```python
CopyEdit
super().speak()
```
This is handy when you want to enhance behavior, not replace it. It's like adding your own guitar solo to an inherited song. OOP lets you remix responsibly.

14.

Want to share behavior between different animals? Inheritance is your jam. All animals might `eat()`, `sleep()`, or `make_sound()`. Subclasses like `Dog`, `Cat`, or `Bird` implement specifics. This lets you write reusable code that applies across many types. Your Animal class becomes a base class or **superclass**. Dogs and cats become **subclasses**. You're building a class family tree.

15.

Sometimes you need **private attributes**. Python doesn't enforce strict privacy, but it lets you hide things with an underscore:

```python
CopyEdit
self._secret = "shh"
```
Or double underscore for name mangling:

```python
CopyEdit
self.__really_hidden = "no peeking"
```
These aren't truly private—but they discourage accidental access. Python trusts you not to be sneaky. It's coding with honor.

16.

Use **properties** to control access:

```python
```

```python
@property
def age(self):
    return self._age
```

This makes `dog.age` act like an attribute but run code behind the scenes. You can also create a setter:

python

```python
@age.setter
def age(self, value):
    if value >= 0:
        self._age = value
```

Properties give you both power and safety. Clean interface, controlled logic.

17.

Want to see all an object's attributes? Use `__dict__`:

python

```python
print(dog.__dict__)
```

This prints a dictionary of attribute names and values. Great for debugging or showing object state. Want to check if an object has a method? Use `hasattr(obj, "method_name")`. Python gives you reflection without the headache. Objects can even inspect themselves. Very meta.

18.

You can also check class type with `isinstance()`:

python

```python
isinstance(fido, Dog)
```

This tells you whether an object belongs to a specific class. Want to know if one class inherits from another? Use `issubclass(Dog, Animal)`. This is perfect for building tools, validators, or frameworks. Python gives you the introspection powers of a philosopher. Go forth and ponder.

19.

Your challenge:

- Create a class `Car` with attributes `make`, `model`, and `year`

- Add a method `start()` that prints "Vroom!"

- Add a `__str__()` method that shows the full name

- Create two cars and call `start()` on both
  You've just built your first car factory. Python: now with horsepower.

20.
Let's recap. Classes let you create blueprints. Objects are instances of those classes. You store attributes (data) and write methods (actions). With inheritance, you share behavior. With encapsulation, you protect it. Object-Oriented Programming gives your code structure, personality, and serious reusability.

21.
You've now crossed into Python 2.0 territory—code that isn't just functional, but **designed**. You can model anything: a store, a game, a spaceship, a llama farm. Objects give your logic a home, a name, and a sense of purpose. You don't just write code. You build **systems**.

22.
Next up: **Advanced Python Tricks – Slicing, Packing, and Unpacking Your Brain**. You'll learn how to manipulate data like a chef with a very sharp knife. It's time to master lists, tuples, and arguments with style. Let's go full ninja.

Chapter 15: Working with APIs – Talking to the Internet Like a Pro

1.
You've made it past functions, classes, and even file handling—but now it's time to unlock your Python program's passport and send it out into the world. How? With **APIs**, short for **Application Programming Interfaces**—a fancy name for how programs talk to each other. APIs let you access data from the web, control smart devices, fetch cat facts, check the weather, and more—all without leaving your Python code. You don't scrape websites anymore; you politely ask APIs for the goods. Think of APIs as digital vending machines: you insert a request and get a neatly packaged response. And Python? Python knows exactly which buttons to press. Talking to the internet has never been so polite—or so powerful.

2.
To work with APIs in Python, your best friend is the `requests` library. It's not part of the standard library, but it's so popular it might as well be. If you don't already have it, just run:

```bash
CopyEdit
pip install requests
```
Once it's installed, you can send a basic GET request like this:

```python
CopyEdit
import requests
response = requests.get("https://api.example.com/data")
```
Now your Python script just made a virtual phone call. And the API answered.

3.

Let's inspect that response.

```python
CopyEdit
print(response.status_code)
print(response.text)
```
The `status_code` tells you if the call was successful—200 means "all good," while 404 means "whoops, not found." The `text` property contains the raw response—usually in **JSON** format. To actually use that data, convert it using `.json()`:

```python
CopyEdit
data = response.json()
print(data)
```
Now your code has structured data—ready to rock.

4.

So, what's a **GET request**? It's the most common kind of API call—it asks for data. Think of it as saying, "Hey, API, gimme that info." You can also send **parameters** with your request:

```python
CopyEdit
params = {"user": "alice", "id": 123}
requests.get(url, params=params)
```
The URL will look like: `https://api.site.com?user=alice&id=123`. Python handles the encoding for you—no need to wrestle with question marks and ampersands.

5.

Want to send data to the API instead of just getting it? That's where **POST requests** come in.

```python
CopyEdit
payload = {"name": "Ada", "email": "ada@example.com"}
response = requests.post("https://api.site.com/register",
json=payload)
```

Now you're submitting data—like a web form. You can also use `data=payload` for form-encoded data, but `json=payload` is more common for APIs. POST is like handing the server a filled-out form. And sometimes it gives you a receipt in return.

6.
Let's look at a real API example:

```python
CopyEdit
response = requests.get("https://api.agify.io/?
name=Michael")
```
This fun little API predicts a name's age. The response might be:

```json
CopyEdit
{"name":"Michael","age":69,"count":12345}
```
You just guessed someone's age over the internet. Welcome to Python-powered ESP.

7.
Need to pass in **headers** (like API keys or content types)? No problem:

```python
CopyEdit
headers = {"Authorization": "Bearer YOUR_API_KEY"}
requests.get(url, headers=headers)
```
Many APIs require authentication—and this is how you provide it. Some use API keys in the headers, others in the query parameters. Always check the API's documentation. Python's `requests` handles both styles like a champ.

8.
Speaking of API keys—treat them like your Netflix password. Don't hardcode them in your scripts. Instead, store them in environment variables or a separate config file and load them with `os.environ`:

```python
CopyEdit
import os
api_key = os.environ.get("API_KEY")
```
This protects your credentials, especially when uploading code to GitHub. Safety first. Internet second.

9.
Sometimes APIs limit how many calls you can make—this is called **rate limiting**. If you send too many requests, you might get a `429 Too Many Requests` error. Some APIs ask you to wait between requests or provide a retry window. Always be a polite API citizen. Spamming

endpoints is a fast track to getting blocked. Reading the docs is like reading the terms of use — except this one can ban your code.

10.

Want to check if your request was successful? Use `response.ok`:

```python
CopyEdit
if response.ok:
    print("Success!")
else:
    print("Something went wrong:", response.status_code)
```

This boolean saves you from parsing status codes manually. Combine it with exception handling for bulletproof API logic. Robust code is happy code.

11.

Let's do a full example:

```python
CopyEdit
import requests
def get_joke():
    url = "https://official-joke-api.appspot.com/jokes/random"
    response = requests.get(url)
    if response.ok:
        joke = response.json()
        print(joke["setup"])
        print(joke["punchline"])
    else:
        print("No laughs today.")
```

You just built a one-click comedy machine. Internet + Python = joy.

12.

Let's talk about errors. Use `try/except` to catch `requests.exceptions`:

```python
CopyEdit
try:
    response = requests.get(url, timeout=5)
except requests.exceptions.RequestException as e:
    print(f"API error: {e}")
```

Timeouts, bad URLs, server errors—it's all fair game. Catching these makes your code more resilient. The internet can be messy. Your code shouldn't be.

13.

Want to save the API response to a file?

```python
CopyEdit
with open("data.json", "w") as file:
    json.dump(response.json(), file)
```

Now you've got offline access. You can also read it back later with `json.load()`. This is perfect for caching, backups, or sending API results to your team. Or your cat. We don't judge.

14.

Sometimes the API response is paginated—meaning you only get part of the data at a time. You'll need to fetch multiple pages using parameters like `?page=2`. Loop until you hit an empty response or a flag indicating the end. Python is great at automation. Once you understand the structure, you can page through data like a web-crawling ninja.

15.

Need to upload a file?

```python
CopyEdit
files = {"file": open("report.pdf", "rb")}
requests.post(url, files=files)
```

This sends your file as part of the request. APIs that accept uploads will tell you exactly what format they expect. Python makes it as easy as dragging and dropping—code style.

16.

Some APIs use more advanced **authentication** like OAuth. For that, use libraries like `oauthlib`, `requests-oauthlib`, or platform-specific SDKs. Authentication is the bouncer at the club door—you need the right ID. It's more setup but totally doable. Once you're authenticated, APIs treat your code like a VIP.

17.

Let's get creative: build a Python program that checks the weather.

```python
CopyEdit
city = input("City: ")
response = requests.get(f"https://wttr.in/{city}?format=3")
print(response.text)
```

Boom—weather in one line. This is the kind of magic Python makes easy. Now go build your own weather dashboard or umbrella reminder bot.

18.

APIs are everywhere—news, sports, finance, memes, maps, food, space. NASA even has an open API with pictures from Mars. You can automate tasks, build dashboards, send alerts, or even generate art. APIs connect your Python code to a universe of possibilities. If it exists online, there's probably an API for it.

19.

Your challenge:

- Pick a public API (jokes, quotes, or dog pics)

- Fetch and display a random item

- Add error handling

- Save the response locally
  This combines requests, file I/O, and logic. You've now built a mini app. That's more than most tutorial coders ever do.

20.

Let's recap. APIs are how Python talks to other systems. You use `requests` to send GET or POST calls, with headers, parameters, and JSON data. Handle errors gracefully. Use `.json()` to work with structured data. And always read the docs. With practice, you'll talk to APIs like a native.

21.

You're no longer limited to local logic. Your code can reach out, grab information, interact with other platforms, and become part of something bigger. This is where your Python journey leaves the desktop and joins the cloud. APIs are your bridge. Now you know how to cross it—like a pro.

22.

Next up: **Web Scraping – When APIs Ghost You**. Because sometimes, there's no API… and you still want the data. We'll explore tools like BeautifulSoup and requests to safely and smartly extract data from real websites. Let's scrape without scorn.

Chapter 16: Regular Expressions – Text Searching with a Secret Code

1.

If you've ever wanted to find a phone number in a mountain of text, validate email addresses with wizardry, or filter log files like a ninja, you're about to meet your new best friend: **Regular**

Expressions. Think of regex as a secret language that lets you describe patterns in text with almost supernatural precision. To outsiders, it looks like cat-on-a-keyboard gibberish. But to those in the know, it's pure textual magic. In Python, regex is powered by the `re` module. It turns your humble string matching into a flexible, blazing-fast pattern-matching engine. Prepare to search, slice, and scrutinize text like a spy. Let's crack the code.

2.

Start by importing the module:

```python
CopyEdit
import re
```

Now you can use `re.search()`, `re.match()`, `re.findall()`, and more. Each has its own purpose, but they all rely on **patterns**. A pattern is a string of special symbols, letters, and digits that defines what you're looking for. You're not just matching exact words—you're matching rules. It's like building a detector that beeps when a match walks by.

3.

Let's begin with `re.search()`:

```python
CopyEdit
result = re.search(r"cat", "The catalog is full.")
```

If the pattern is found anywhere in the string, `re.search()` returns a match object. If not, it returns `None`. Notice the **raw string** prefix `r"..."`—this tells Python to treat backslashes literally, which is essential in regex. Without it, your pattern will collapse in a backslash tornado. Always use `r"..."` when writing regex patterns in Python.

4.

What does `r"cat"` actually match? Just the string "cat"—easy. But what if you wanted to match any digit? Use `\d`.

```python
CopyEdit
re.search(r"\d", "Room 7B")
```

This matches the 7. `\d` is shorthand for "any digit from 0 to 9." Other handy shorthands: `\w` matches word characters (letters, digits, underscores), `\s` matches whitespace, and their uppercase versions (`\D`, `\W`, `\S`) match the opposites. Regex is polite like that—it always brings an evil twin.

5.

Use **character classes** with square brackets to match specific characters:

```python
CopyEdit
```

```python
re.search(r"[aeiou]", "Python")
```
This finds the first vowel. Want to match anything except those? Use a caret:

```python
CopyEdit
re.search(r"[^aeiou]", "Python")
```
That matches the first consonant. Character classes are like creating your own mini-alphabets. Need digits, symbols, or specific ranges? This is your toolbox.

6.

Want to match more than one character? Use **quantifiers**.

- **+** means "one or more"

- ***** means "zero or more"

- **?** means "zero or one"

- **{n}** means "exactly n"

- **{n,}** means "n or more"

- **{n,m}** means "between n and m"
  For example, **\d+** matches one or more digits. It's like saying, "Give me the whole number, not just a piece."

7.

Let's match a phone number:

```python
CopyEdit
re.search(r"\d{3}-\d{3}-\d{4}", "Call 555-123-4567")
```
This matches U.S. phone numbers with dashes. Want to allow spaces or parentheses? Try:

```python
CopyEdit
r"\(?\d{3}\)?[-\s]?\d{3}[-\s]?\d{4}"
```
Now it matches a variety of formats. Regex gets more powerful the more flexible your patterns become. That power, of course, comes with complexity—but it's worth the effort.

8.

Use **anchors** to control *where* your match occurs:

- **^** means "start of string"

- **$** means "end of string"

```python
CopyEdit
re.search(r"^Hello", "Hello there")   # Matches
re.search(r"world$", "Hello world")   # Matches
```
Anchors help when you only care about beginnings or endings. Regex isn't just *what* you match —it's also *where* you match it.

9.

Want to extract multiple matches? Use `re.findall()`:

```python
CopyEdit
re.findall(r"\d+", "I have 3 cats and 2 dogs.")
```
This returns a list: `['3', '2']`. It finds all non-overlapping matches in the string. Want match objects instead? Use `re.finditer()`—it returns an iterator of match objects with details. You now have options: extract results fast, or examine them deeply. Your text doesn't stand a chance.

10.

Let's extract names:

```python
CopyEdit
text = "Name: Alice, Name: Bob, Name: Charlie"
re.findall(r"Name: (\w+)", text)
```
This returns `['Alice', 'Bob', 'Charlie']`. The parentheses create a **capture group**—they tell regex to "save this part." You can create multiple groups and access them using `match.group(n)` where n is the group number. Groups turn pattern matches into extractable data. You're not just matching—you're mining.

11.

Need to **substitute** text? Use `re.sub()`:

```python
CopyEdit
re.sub(r"\d+", "[number]", "I have 2 apples and 5
oranges.")
```
Now it says, "I have [number] apples and [number] oranges." You can also use \1, \2, etc. in the replacement to reuse matched groups. Think of it as a find-and-replace engine with X-ray vision. Text transformation becomes surgical. And you're the regex scalpel.

12.

What if you want to split a string by something fancy, like multiple punctuation marks?

```python
```

```
re.split(r"[,;.!]", "One, two; three. four!")
```

This returns a list: `['One', ' two', ' three', ' four', '']`. It's like `.split()` but smarter. Great for tokenizing text or preprocessing messy data. Regex doesn't just find—it divides.

13.

Let's validate an email address:

python

```
pattern = r"^[\w\.-]+@[\w\.-]+\.\w{2,4}$"
```

This matches most email formats—though it won't win a gold medal in Olympic-level validation. Email regex can get insane fast, so use this for casual use only. For stricter checking, consider built-in libraries or email-parsing modules. But for everyday input? This gets the job done—and looks cool doing it.

14.

Want to test your pattern? Use online tools like regex101.com. You get real-time feedback, explanations, and sample test cases. It's like regex karaoke—try a few patterns, see what works, and adjust on the fly. Even seasoned pros test before they code. There's no shame in debugging your squiggles.

15.

Let's use named groups for readability:

python

```
pattern = r"Name: (?P<name>\w+), Age: (?P<age>\d+)"
```

Now you can access results with `match.group("name")` and `match.group("age")`. This makes your code easier to read, especially with complex patterns. Named groups are regex for grownups. You're now classy and precise.

16.

Need to match a literal character that's normally special? Escape it with a backslash:

python

```
re.search(r"\$", "Price: $99")
```

Regex treats characters like `. * + ? ( ) { } [ ] | \` as special. To match them literally, you need to escape. It's like telling regex, "Chill—I just want the dollar sign, not the end of the world." Escaping is essential to avoid unintended matches.

17.

Let's write a function that extracts all hashtags from a tweet:

```python
CopyEdit
def extract_hashtags(tweet):
    return re.findall(r"#\w+", tweet)
```
Now `extract_hashtags("Loving #Python and #regex today!")`
returns `['#Python', '#regex']`. You've just built a social media tool in one line. Your pattern-matching game is strong. And your tweets are ready for analysis.

18.
Regex is great, but also easy to overuse. Don't turn every string task into a pattern if `.split()`, `.replace()`, or `.startswith()` will do. Regex is for **complex** patterns —like validation, extraction, or parsing. Think of it as your laser scalpel, not your butter knife. Use it when you need precision, not every time you slice a string.

19.
Your challenge:

- Write a function that extracts all dates in the format MM/DD/YYYY from a string

- Then substitute them with [DATE]

- Use `re.findall()` and `re.sub()`
  This reinforces pattern matching, grouping, and substitution. You've just built a mini date sanitizer. It's regex with responsibility.

20.
Let's recap. Regular expressions are pattern languages for text. You use the `re` module to search, match, split, substitute, and extract. Patterns use symbols, quantifiers, character classes, and anchors. Groups let you extract parts. Named groups make it readable. With a little practice, regex becomes second nature.

21.
Regex is one of the most powerful tools in Python—and one of the most misunderstood. But now, you don't fear the backslashes. You wield them. You can clean messy data, validate user input, and turn unstructured text into structured gold. You're not just writing code anymore. You're deciphering the Matrix.

22.
Next up: **The Pythonic Way – Writing Clean, Readable, and Elegant Code**. You've learned the tools—now let's learn the style. We'll talk about conventions, list comprehensions, idiomatic code, and the beauty of "there's a better way." Let's go from good to great.

Chapter 17: Web Scraping – Python, the Data Thief (for Good)

1.

Let's be clear: **web scraping is not illegal**—unless you make it weird. If the data is publicly available, and you're not crashing the site or violating terms of service, then it's just **automated browsing**. Think of web scraping as reading a website with superhuman speed and perfect memory. You're not stealing—you're **liberating data** that's already there. With Python, scraping becomes surprisingly easy—and dangerously addictive. You'll need two tools: `requests` to fetch the page, and `BeautifulSoup` to decode the HTML like a digital archaeologist. By the end of this chapter, you'll be able to pull down quotes, headlines, or even... cat facts. Let's scrape responsibly.

2.

Install BeautifulSoup and requests with pip:

```bash
CopyEdit
pip install beautifulsoup4 requests
```

These two packages are the peanut butter and jelly of web scraping. Requests grabs the HTML; BeautifulSoup lets you parse and extract what you need. It's like having a browser and magnifying glass rolled into one. Once installed, you're ready to start crawling (the fun kind).

Just remember: with great power comes great politeness. Always obey `robots.txt` files and don't overload servers.

3.

Let's fetch a page:

```python
CopyEdit
import requests
from bs4 import BeautifulSoup

url = "https://quotes.toscrape.com"
response = requests.get(url)
soup = BeautifulSoup(response.text, "html.parser")
```

Now `soup` contains the entire HTML of the page—ready for you to slice and dice. It's like a big pot of soup—hot, messy, and full of hidden ingredients.

4.

Want to extract all the quotes?

```python
CopyEdit
quotes = soup.find_all("span", class_="text")
for quote in quotes:
    print(quote.text)
```
This grabs all <span> elements with class "text". BeautifulSoup's find_all() method is your treasure map. You can search by tag name, class, ID, or a combination. Need the author too? Just look for the adjacent class.

5.
Let's get authors too:

```python
CopyEdit
authors = soup.find_all("small", class_="author")
```
Now loop through both quotes and authors:

```python
CopyEdit
for q, a in zip(quotes, authors):
    print(f"{q.text} — {a.text}")
```
You've just built a mini quote generator. Hallmark should be worried.

6.
What if you want to scrape multiple pages? Look for the "Next" button:

```python
CopyEdit
next_page = soup.find("li", class_="next")
```
Grab its link and follow it:

```python
CopyEdit
url = "https://quotes.toscrape.com" + next_page.a["href"]
```
Repeat the process until next_page is None. You've officially entered **pagination** territory — scraper level: intermediate. Python loops + HTML structure = scraping nirvana.

7.
Let's loop through pages:

```python
CopyEdit
while next_page:
    response = requests.get(url)
    soup = BeautifulSoup(response.text, "html.parser")
```

```
# scrape here
next_page = soup.find("li", class_="next")
url = "https://quotes.toscrape.com" +
next_page.a["href"] if next_page else None
```

This loops through every page, scraping like a polite robot. Bonus points if you sleep between requests to avoid being a digital pest. Python never rushes data art.

8.

Want to scrape job listings, blog headlines, or weather reports? Same process. Inspect the site in your browser (right-click > Inspect) to find the HTML structure. Look for divs, spans, classes, IDs — anything consistent. The hardest part of scraping is figuring out where the data hides. Once you've mapped the site's skeleton, you can automate the entire thing. You're now officially a web detective.

9.

Let's extract links:

python
CopyEdit
```python
links = soup.find_all("a")
for link in links:
    print(link.get("href"))
```

`.get("href")` pulls the URL from the anchor tag. Want only external links? Filter by those starting with `"http"`. You're not just reading content — you're mapping the web.

10.

Scraping tables? Easy peasy.

python
CopyEdit
```python
rows = soup.find_all("tr")
for row in rows:
    cols = row.find_all("td")
    data = [col.text.strip() for col in cols]
    print(data)
```

Tables are structured gold. Whether it's sports stats, currency rates, or pizza toppings — HTML tables are your best friends.

11.

Let's clean up some text. Use `.strip()` to remove whitespace.

python
CopyEdit
```python
quote.text.strip()
```

You can also use `re.sub()` (remember regex?) to clean up unwanted characters. BeautifulSoup is flexible, but you'll often need to post-process the data. Clean input = clean output. Scraping is 50% extraction, 50% sanitation.

12.
Want to scrape images?

python
CopyEdit
```python
images = soup.find_all("img")
for img in images:
    print(img["src"])
```
Download them with requests:

python
CopyEdit
```python
img_data = requests.get(img_url).content
with open("image.jpg", "wb") as f:
    f.write(img_data)
```
Boom—you're now a Python-powered photo downloader. (Still legally and ethically, of course.)

13.
Don't forget about headers:

python
CopyEdit
```python
headers = {"User-Agent": "Mozilla/5.0"}
requests.get(url, headers=headers)
```
Some sites block scrapers unless they see a valid browser user agent. Sending headers helps you blend in. Python, the stealthy web surfer.

14.
If a site uses JavaScript to load content, BeautifulSoup won't help. You'll need **Selenium** or **Playwright** to render JavaScript like a browser. These tools let you click buttons, scroll pages, and wait for elements to appear. But they're slower and heavier than BeautifulSoup. Use them only when necessary—scraping static HTML is much easier. Remember: just because a site looks empty doesn't mean the data isn't there. JavaScript often hides it behind the curtain.

15.
Let's scrape JSON hidden in a script tag.

python
CopyEdit
```python
import json
script = soup.find("script", type="application/ld+json")
```

```python
data = json.loads(script.string)
```
Now you've extracted structured data straight from the source. Some sites offer more JSON in their HTML than their actual APIs. It's like finding buried treasure under the floorboards.

16.
Let's write a scraper that saves quotes to a CSV:

python
CopyEdit
```python
import csv
with open("quotes.csv", "w", newline="") as file:
    writer = csv.writer(file)
    writer.writerow(["Quote", "Author"])
    for q, a in zip(quotes, authors):
        writer.writerow([q.text, a.text])
```
You now have data you can analyze, visualize, or send to your boss with a smug email. Python turns data into deliverables.

17.
How do you know if scraping is allowed? Check `robots.txt`:

python
CopyEdit
```
https://example.com/robots.txt
```
It lists which parts of a site you can scrape. Some sites say "no bots allowed." Respect that. It's like asking for permission before you raid the cookie jar.

18.
Some tips for ethical scraping:

- Don't hammer servers—add `time.sleep()` between requests

- Don't scrape logged-in content

- Don't impersonate users or APIs

- Do cache results when possible

- Do credit the source if sharing data
  Scraping is cool. Being a considerate scraper is cooler.

19.
Your challenge:

- Pick a website with a list (books, articles, products)

- Scrape the title, price, or rating

- Save to CSV

- Bonus: scrape multiple pages
  You've now built a data pipeline. Welcome to real-world coding.

20.

Let's recap. Web scraping uses `requests` to fetch pages and `BeautifulSoup` to parse them. You use tags, classes, and IDs to find elements. Then clean, extract, and maybe store the data. Handle pagination, headers, and delays with care. For dynamic sites, use Selenium. For ethical scraping—respect robots.txt.

21.

You've just learned how to extract structured data from unstructured chaos. You don't have to wait for APIs or prebuilt datasets anymore. With a little HTML sleuthing and Python, the web is your oyster. Or rather, your open buffet. Just bring your scraper fork.

22.

Next up: **Testing and Debugging – Squashing Bugs with Science**. Because even perfect scrapers break. You'll learn how to test your code, catch bugs, and debug like Sherlock with a keyboard. Let's de-crash everything.

Chapter 18: Automation – Make Your Computer Do the Boring Stuff

1.

Let's admit it: the modern world runs on repetition. Copy this. Paste that. Rename a hundred files. Fill in a spreadsheet. Email your manager… again. What if Python could do all that while you sip coffee and judge others for still working manually? That's where **automation** steps in—Python's specialty. Say goodbye to busywork and hello to laziness with dignity.

2.

Automation isn't just coding—it's supercharging your **daily workflow**. From renaming files and moving folders to scraping reports and sending emails, Python can do it all. And it'll never complain, call in sick, or click the wrong thing out of boredom. The goal here is simple: **write once, relax forever**. Or until your script breaks. Either way, it's better than clicking 1,000 times in a spreadsheet. Let's start small and scale fast. Your time is too valuable for manual labor.

3.

One of the simplest automations is renaming files.

```python
CopyEdit
import os

for filename in os.listdir("my_folder"):
    if filename.endswith(".txt"):
        new_name = filename.replace(" ", "_")
        os.rename(f"my_folder/{filename}", f"my_folder/{new_name}")
```

Now every `.txt` file in the folder has underscores instead of spaces. Boom—manual renaming eliminated. You just saved twenty minutes (and some wrist pain).

4.

Let's automate **file organization**.

```python
CopyEdit
import shutil

for file in os.listdir("downloads"):
    if file.endswith(".jpg"):
        shutil.move(f"downloads/{file}", f"images/{file}")
```

This script scans your download folder and moves images to a subfolder. You can extend this to PDFs, ZIPs, and Excel sheets. Python, the digital butler, is happy to tidy up after you. It doesn't even need a raise.

5.

Now let's automate **opening programs or websites**.

```python
CopyEdit
import webbrowser

webbrowser.open("https://www.python.org")
```

This opens a webpage in your default browser. You can even open multiple tabs at once, making it perfect for your daily startup ritual. Want to automate your morning routine? Open weather, email, news, and memes in one go.

6.

What about automating **emails**?

```python
CopyEdit
import smtplib
```

```python
from email.message import EmailMessage

msg = EmailMessage()
msg.set_content("Hello, this is automated.")
msg["Subject"] = "Python says hi"
msg["From"] = "you@example.com"
msg["To"] = "friend@example.com"

with smtplib.SMTP("smtp.gmail.com", 587) as smtp:
    smtp.starttls()
    smtp.login("you@example.com", "password")
    smtp.send_message(msg)
```
Warning: never hardcode passwords—use environment variables or secret managers. Python doesn't judge, but Gmail might.

7.

Let's generate PDFs automatically.

python
CopyEdit
```python
from fpdf import FPDF

pdf = FPDF()
pdf.add_page()
pdf.set_font("Arial", size=12)
pdf.cell(200, 10, txt="This was generated by Python!",
ln=True)
pdf.output("auto_doc.pdf")
```
Now you're auto-authoring documents like a boss. Add tables, headers, even graphs—and automate your reporting.

8.

Want to auto-fill forms or click buttons? Meet **pyautogui**:

python
CopyEdit
```python
import pyautogui
pyautogui.write("Hello, world!", interval=0.1)
pyautogui.press("enter")
```
Now your script types and hits Enter for you. You can also move the mouse, take screenshots, and click buttons. It's like giving your computer a ghost hand. Use responsibly—and maybe don't prank coworkers. (Unless it's hilarious.)

9.

Let's schedule tasks.

```python
CopyEdit
import schedule
import time

def greet():
    print("Time to stand up and stretch!")

schedule.every(1).hours.do(greet)

while True:
    schedule.run_pending()
    time.sleep(1)
```
Now your computer becomes a life coach. Gentle reminders, automated.

10.

Need to automate downloading files?

```python
CopyEdit
import requests

url = "https://example.com/report.pdf"
r = requests.get(url)
with open("report.pdf", "wb") as f:
    f.write(r.content)
```
This fetches a file and saves it—no browser needed. Python: now with download manager mode enabled.

11.

How about watching a folder for changes?

```python
CopyEdit
from watchdog.observers import Observer
from watchdog.events import FileSystemEventHandler

class Watcher(FileSystemEventHandler):
    def on_modified(self, event):
        print(f"{event.src_path} was modified!")
```

```python
observer = Observer()
observer.schedule(Watcher(), path="my_folder",
recursive=False)
observer.start()
```
Now your script detects file edits like a digital guard dog. Great for real-time workflows or automating responses.

12.
You can also control Excel with Python.

```python
CopyEdit
import openpyxl

wb = openpyxl.Workbook()
ws = wb.active
ws["A1"] = "Automated entry"
wb.save("spreadsheet.xlsx")
```
Say goodbye to manual entry. Automate reports, inventory sheets, or even grades. Python + Excel = unstoppable duo.

13.
Need to monitor websites for changes?

```python
CopyEdit
import hashlib

def get_hash(url):
    content = requests.get(url).text
    return hashlib.md5(content.encode()).hexdigest()
```
Compare hashes over time to detect content changes. Alert yourself if something updates. You just built a tiny web monitoring bot. Security analysts everywhere would high-five you.

14.
Want to tweet automatically?

```python
CopyEdit
import tweepy

# Authenticate and tweet using API keys
# (Requires setting up a Twitter Developer account)
```

With the right setup, your Python script becomes your social media manager. Schedule tweets, respond to mentions, or post your latest blog. Python's got your brand's back.

15.
You can even automate backups:

```python
CopyEdit
import shutil


shutil.copy("data.db", "backup/data_backup.db")
```
Set this to run daily and you've got your own low-budget IT department. Backups = peace of mind. Automate them before you lose something important.

16.
For real productivity, combine these tools.

- Scrape data

- Write it to Excel

- Email it to your boss

- Archive it to a backup folder
  Boom—four hours of work done in one script. Python doesn't just automate tasks. It automates **processes**.

17.
You can even auto-respond to keyboard shortcuts using libraries like `keyboard` or `autohotkey`.

```python
CopyEdit
import keyboard


keyboard.add_hotkey("ctrl+alt+h", lambda: print("Hello!"))
keyboard.wait("esc")
```
Create instant tools that trigger with a keystroke. It's like giving yourself digital superpowers.

18.
Your challenge:

- Create a folder cleaner

- Move files into subfolders by extension

- Run it every day

- Log the actions to a file
  You now have a utility script that saves time and brings order to chaos. Congratulations, you're now the office wizard.

19.

Let's recap. Automation is about turning manual tasks into repeatable scripts. Python makes this insanely easy with libraries like `os`, `shutil`, `requests`, `pyautogui`, `openpyxl`, and more. You can rename files, scrape websites, send emails, and launch programs—all with a few lines of code. Whether it's office work, creative projects, or digital housecleaning, automation helps you scale yourself. Write once. Reuse often. Reclaim your time.

20.

Automation isn't just about efficiency—it's about **freedom**. Freeing your mind to solve new problems. Freeing your hands from mindless tasks. Freeing your time for better things (or naps—we support naps). Python doesn't just automate—it **liberates**. And that's what makes it so powerful.

21.

You now know how to make your computer do the boring stuff. You've become the conductor of your digital orchestra. Need a report? Done. Need to send 300 emails? Easy. Want your computer to water your plants? Okay, maybe not… yet. But you get the idea.

22.

Next up: **Testing and Debugging – Squashing Bugs with Science**. Because no automation is complete without a little quality control. We'll cover test cases, error messages, breakpoints, and fixing things without screaming. Let's make sure your lazy scripts are also reliable ones.

Chapter 19: Virtual Environments – Keeping Your Dependencies in Line

1.

Picture this: You build a Python project using version 3.9 and package X v1.4. Six months later, you start a new project needing X v2.0. Suddenly, your old project breaks. Welcome to **dependency hell**—where old packages cry, new ones scream, and your global Python installation turns into a junk drawer. The solution? **Virtual environments**. They let each project live in its own bubble, like a software terrarium. Clean, isolated, drama-free development.

2.

So, what exactly is a virtual environment? It's a self-contained directory that includes its own

Python executable and a local site-packages directory. It lets you install packages *just* for one project, without affecting others. No more worrying if upgrading Flask will break your Django blog. No more "it works on my machine" excuses. Every project gets its own personalized Python world. And yes—it's way easier than it sounds.

3.

The most common tool is `venv`, built right into Python 3.

```bash
CopyEdit
python -m venv myenv
```

This creates a new folder named `myenv`, containing everything you need. It doesn't touch your global Python or affect your system. Inside, you'll find a `bin` or `Scripts` folder (depending on your OS), a `lib` directory, and a `pyvenv.cfg` config file. Congratulations—you've just created an ecosystem.

4.

Now you need to **activate** it.

- On macOS/Linux:
  ```bash
  CopyEdit
  source myenv/bin/activate
  ```

-

- On Windows:
  ```bash
  CopyEdit
  myenv\Scripts\activate
  ```

-

Your terminal prompt will change to include `(myenv)` —a reminder that you're now operating inside the Matrix. Any package you install from this point forward goes into the environment, not the global Python setup. Welcome to isolated bliss.

5.

Let's test it.

```bash
CopyEdit
pip install requests
```

Now run:

```bash
CopyEdit
pip list
```

You'll see only the packages you've installed in *this* environment. Want to verify even further? Try `which python` (mac/Linux) or `where python` (Windows). It'll point to the local `myenv` version. Boom—proof you're sandboxed.

6.

To leave the environment, just type:

```bash
CopyEdit
deactivate
```

You'll return to your system's global Python. It's like leaving a fancy Airbnb and going back to your cluttered apartment. But the good news? Your environment stays frozen in time, waiting for your return. No judgment. No conflicts.

7.

So why bother with all this? One word: **control**. Different projects often need different dependencies—or different versions of the same ones. Without environments, installing one thing can break another. With them, your project dependencies are locked in. Like a chef with separate spice racks for each recipe, Python now cooks clean.

8.

Want to recreate an environment somewhere else?

Use `pip freeze` to save your installed packages:

```bash
CopyEdit
pip freeze > requirements.txt
```

Then share or store that file. To recreate the environment on another machine (or the future), run:

```bash
CopyEdit
pip install -r requirements.txt
```

It's like version control for your dependencies. Every team member gets the same recipe.

9.

You can name your environment anything, but conventions help. Many devs name it `venv` or `.venv`. The dot version keeps it hidden from version control tools by default. You typically don't commit your environment folder to Git—just the `requirements.txt`. This keeps your repo lean, clean, and reproducible. Trust us—future-you will be grateful.

10.

Need to manage *lots* of environments? Try **virtualenvwrapper** (Linux/macOS) or **Pipenv/ Poetry** (all platforms). These tools offer shortcut commands and better dependency management.

- `pipenv` handles both environments and dependencies in one go

- `poetry` adds versioning, publishing, and other advanced features
  Start with `venv`, but know there's a whole ecosystem if you want more bells and whistles. Pick your flavor based on project needs.

11.

Want to automate activation? Many IDEs (like VS Code or PyCharm) detect virtual environments automatically. They switch environments when you open the project folder. You can also configure `.vscode/settings.json` to point to your preferred interpreter. Less typing, more doing. IDEs and venvs are better together.

12.

Running scripts inside a virtual environment is easy:

```bash
CopyEdit
python script.py
```

As long as the environment is activated, your script uses its packages. Want to schedule it with cron or Task Scheduler? Just be sure the virtual environment is activated in your job's context. Think of the activation like stretching before a run—small step, big results.

13.

Here's a cool trick: activate an environment from within a script using `subprocess`:

```python
CopyEdit
import subprocess
subprocess.run("source venv/bin/activate && python
myscript.py", shell=True)
```

This is useful when chaining environments or running automated jobs. Still, the cleanest approach is to activate manually or via shell scripts. Respect the venv, and it will respect you.

14.

How do you tell which packages are installed where? Try `pip show packagename`. It tells you the location, version, and dependencies of that package. If you're inside a venv, the paths will be local. If you're not, the paths are global. Always know where your dependencies live. It's the Python equivalent of knowing where your towel is.

15.
Your challenge:

- Create a new virtual environment

- Install `requests` and `beautifulsoup4`

- Freeze the dependencies

- Delete the environment

- Recreate it from `requirements.txt`
  You've just mastered the full lifecycle. From setup to teardown and rebirth. Python DevOps level: unlocked.

16.
You can also install packages in editable mode for local development:

```bash
CopyEdit
pip install -e .
```
This is great for working on your own packages while testing them inside a virtual environment. Think of it as live feedback. Great for debugging, development, and living your best modular life.

17.
Need to upgrade a package inside a venv?

```bash
CopyEdit
pip install --upgrade packagename
```
This won't affect other projects, which is the whole point of using environments. Test upgrades without fear. Break things in peace. It's your virtual sandbox.

18.
Want to get fancy? Use `.env` files and `python-dotenv` to load environment variables securely.

```bash
CopyEdit
pip install python-dotenv
```

You can now keep API keys, tokens, and secrets out of your codebase. Combine this with `venv` for fully isolated, secure projects. Clean structure. Happy automation. Better sleep.

19.
Virtual environments aren't just a best practice—they're a **requirement** for serious Python development. Any real-world project with dependencies *must* use a venv. Otherwise, it's just a ticking time bomb waiting for a library update. Whether you're working solo or with a team, reproducibility matters. Venvs are your safety bubble. Respect the bubble.

20.
Let's recap. Virtual environments isolate dependencies, prevent version conflicts, and allow you to manage projects cleanly. They're created with `venv`, activated with `source`, and frozen with `pip freeze`. You can recreate environments anywhere with `requirements.txt`. Tools like Pipenv and Poetry take it further. This is Python with guardrails—and you're now driving in the fast lane.

21.
You've unlocked a vital part of the Python pro's toolkit. Your code is portable, your projects are cleaner, and you're protected from global chaos. You no longer live in fear of the dreaded "works on my machine." With virtual environments, **every machine can be your machine**. Whether you're scripting, scraping, or shipping software—you're doing it right.

22.
Next up: **Testing and Debugging – Squashing Bugs with Science**. Because now that your environments are perfect, your code deserves to be too. Let's find the flaws, fix the failures, and make bugs wish they'd never hatched. Bring your magnifying glass—it's detective time.

Chapter 20: Testing & Debugging – Because Bugs Are Eternal

1.
You write your code. You run it. And then... nothing. Or worse—**something weird**. Congratulations, you've officially met your first bug. No matter how perfect your logic or poetic your functions, bugs will find you. They're the uninvited guests of every software party. But instead of panicking, you're going to squash them with Python-powered science. Welcome to the world of **testing and debugging**—a place where your code goes from "probably works" to "definitely works."

2.
Let's start with the simplest and most underrated tool: `print()`.

```python
CopyEdit
print("Got here!")
print("Variable x =", x)
```
Sprinkling these throughout your code helps you trace logic, spot unexpected values, and ensure flow. It's quick, dirty, and surprisingly effective. Think of `print()` as your code's diary. But remember: **delete or comment them out** when you're done. Or your logs will read like a desperate cry for help.

3.

For more structure, use **logging**.

```python
CopyEdit
import logging
logging.basicConfig(level=logging.DEBUG)
logging.debug("This is a debug message")
```
Logging lets you record messages at different severity levels: DEBUG, INFO, WARNING, ERROR, CRITICAL. Unlike `print()`, logs can be turned off, filtered, or redirected to files. You can also log timestamps and line numbers. It's the grown-up version of `print()` — with less shame and more control.

4.

Next up: the **traceback**. When your code crashes, Python politely leaves behind a trail of breadcrumbs. This includes the file, line number, function name, and exact error. Don't panic — **read it**. Tracebacks are your friends. They tell you *where* things went wrong and *why*. Learn to love them like an honest critic.

5.

Common Python errors include:

- `NameError`: You used a variable that doesn't exist

- `TypeError`: You used a value in the wrong way (like adding a string to an int)

- `IndexError`: You tried to access a list index that isn't there

- `KeyError`: You accessed a dictionary key that doesn't exist

- `AttributeError`: You called a method on the wrong type
  Recognizing these helps you fix them faster. Like knowing your enemies' names before battle.

6.

Want more power? Try the **Python Debugger**, aka `pdb`.

```python
CopyEdit
import pdb; pdb.set_trace()
```
This pauses your program and opens an interactive shell. You can inspect variables, step through lines, and explore your code mid-crash. Use n to go to the next line, c to continue, and q to quit. It's like Matrix bullet-time for debugging. Slow down the chaos and study the scene.

7.

Use `try/except` blocks to catch and handle errors gracefully:

```python
CopyEdit
try:
    result = 10 / 0
except ZeroDivisionError:
    print("You can't divide by zero, my dude.")
```
This keeps your program from crashing—and gives users a friendly message instead of a stack trace meltdown. Just don't abuse it by catching **everything** and saying "Oops." That's not debugging. That's hiding the evidence.

8.

Now let's talk **testing**. Testing is how you prove your code works—**before** a user breaks it. Start with simple, repeatable **assertions**:

```python
CopyEdit
assert 2 + 2 == 4
```
If the condition is false, Python raises an `AssertionError`. This is a quick sanity check—great for logic gates and mini-validations. If your code passes, it moves on. If not, it explodes early—before bad data spreads like a virus.

9.

For real projects, use Python's built-in **unittest** framework.

```python
CopyEdit
import unittest

class MathTest(unittest.TestCase):
    def test_addition(self):
        self.assertEqual(2 + 2, 4)
```
Run it with:

```bash
bash
```

```
python -m unittest your_test_file.py
```
Unittest checks your code's behavior, line by line, scenario by scenario. You'll sleep better knowing your functions pass more than just a vibe check.

10.
You can test for errors too:

python
```
with self.assertRaises(ZeroDivisionError):
    divide(10, 0)
```
This ensures your code **fails correctly**. Good code isn't just about success. It's about **predictable failure**. Tests catch bad inputs, weird edge cases, and future developer "improvements." You're now building code that holds itself accountable.

11.
Want a simpler way to test? Try **pytest**.

bash
```
pip install pytest
```
Write functions that start with `test_`, then run `pytest` in the terminal.

python
```
def test_add():
    assert 1 + 1 == 2
```
Pytest auto-discovers tests and gives clean, colorful output. It's like `unittest`, but with less boilerplate and more elegance.

12.
Don't just test the "happy path." Test:

- Empty inputs

- Invalid types

- Extreme values

- Boundary conditions

- Incorrect usage
  Good test cases simulate real user behavior—**including mistakes**. The more your tests break, the more your code improves. Write tests to make bugs cry.

13.

Want to test code that uses external APIs or databases? Use **mocking**.

```python
CopyEdit
from unittest.mock import patch
```

This replaces functions or objects with fake ones during testing. Instead of making real API calls, you simulate them. Faster, safer, and cheaper than pinging real servers. Mocking is like dress rehearsal — no risk, just practice.

14.

Make testing part of your workflow. Create a `tests/` folder. Run your tests before every commit. Automate them with CI tools like GitHub Actions or Travis CI. A bug that gets caught in development costs nothing. A bug in production costs your weekend. Invest in testing like it's tech insurance.

15.

Use `coverage.py` to measure how much of your code is tested.

```bash
CopyEdit
pip install coverage
coverage run -m pytest
coverage report
```

This shows you which lines ran — and which were ignored. Aim for 80% or more. But remember — **coverage is not quality**. Test the right things, not just all the things.

16.

Debugging tips that actually work:

- Reproduce the bug consistently

- Reduce the code to a minimal example

- Add `print()` to suspicious lines

- Check your assumptions (is x *really* a list?)

- Read the error message again — slowly
  The goal isn't just to fix it. It's to understand **why** it happened. That's how you prevent it next time.

17.

Here's your challenge:

- Write a function that divides two numbers

- Add tests for valid, zero, and string inputs

- Use `try/except` to handle bad data

- Add logging and assertions
  You've now built testable, fault-tolerant, debug-friendly code. It's not flashy. But it's bulletproof.

18.

Real devs don't fear bugs. They **track them, tag them, and trap them**. They create test cases from every weird edge case a user invents. They write code to prove their code works. They break their own software — on purpose. That's not failure. That's how professionals operate.

19.

Testing isn't a one-time thing. Do it while you code, before you push, after you fix, and every time you refactor. Make it a habit. Good testing culture makes your codebase resilient and your team sleep better. And if you're a solo coder? It makes *you* sleep better too.

20.

Let's recap. Debugging finds problems. Testing prevents them. Use `print()` to trace. Use `pdb` to investigate. Use `unittest` or `pytest` to validate. Mock external stuff, measure coverage, and automate what you can. That's how you build confidence in your code.

21.

Bugs may be eternal, but they are **not immortal**. With the right tools, discipline, and mindset, you'll squash them with flair. You'll go from "what broke?" to "I expected that." Your code isn't just working. It's working *on purpose*.

22.

Next up: **The Finish Line – Building a Real Python Project**. You've got the tools, the skills, and the battle scars. Now let's pull it all together and build something useful. No tutorials. No hand-holding. Just Python and you — let's ship it.

Chapter 21: Data Handling – CSVs, Excel, and Pandas, Oh My!

1.

Welcome to the land of **structured chaos** — where rows and columns roam free, and the mighty spreadsheet rules all. Whether you're managing budgets, analyzing user data, or organizing your Pokémon card collection, working with CSVs and Excel files is a rite of passage. Fortunately, Python was practically born to tame tabular data. And it does so with style, speed, and a wonderfully named library: **pandas**. No, not the bear (though that would be adorable). Pandas is your best friend for reading, writing, cleaning, transforming, slicing, and analyzing data. It takes raw, messy information and makes it beautifully usable. Grab your `.csv` and let's make it sing.

2.

Let's start small—with the humble **CSV** (Comma-Separated Values). A CSV is basically a spreadsheet saved as plain text. Each line is a row, and commas separate the columns. Python has a built-in `csv` module, but we're jumping straight to **pandas** because it's more powerful and way more fun. First, install it:

```bash
CopyEdit
pip install pandas
```
Then import it:

```python
CopyEdit
import pandas as pd
```
And you're ready to wrangle rows like a boss.

3.

Read a CSV with just one line:

```python
CopyEdit
df = pd.read_csv("data.csv")
```
Boom—your CSV is now a **DataFrame**, which is pandas' version of a table. You can view the top rows with `df.head()`, or see the shape with `df.shape`. Want to peek at column names? Try `df.columns`. Pandas gives you a spreadsheet in your terminal—and it doesn't judge your formatting.

4.

Let's explore.

```python
CopyEdit
print(df.info())
print(df.describe())
```
`info()` shows you data types and null values, while `describe()` gives you quick stats (mean, min, max, etc.). This is the fastest way to understand what you're working with. DataFrame methods are designed to give you the **big picture** fast. It's like asking your data, "So... what's your deal?" And getting an honest answer.

5.

Want to access a specific column?

```python
CopyEdit
df["Name"]
```
This returns a **Series**—pandas' version of a single column. Want a specific row? Use `.loc[]` for label-based indexing or `.iloc[]` for position-based:

```python
CopyEdit
df.loc[5]
df.iloc[2]
```
Think of `.loc[]` as "give me row where index is 5," and `.iloc[]` as "give me the third row." It's data slicing with surgical precision.

6.
Let's filter data.

```python
CopyEdit
df[df["Score"] > 90]
```
This returns all rows where the "Score" column is greater than 90. You can also combine conditions:

```python
CopyEdit
df[(df["Score"] > 90) & (df["Grade"] == "A")]
```
Pandas uses `&`, `|`, and `~` for AND, OR, and NOT—just don't forget the parentheses. You're now asking your data questions—and it's answering back.

7.
Want to add a new column?

```python
CopyEdit
df["Passed"] = df["Score"] >= 60
```
Now every row has a Boolean telling you if that student passed. Pandas makes column math easy:

```python
CopyEdit
df["Bonus"] = df["Score"] * 1.1
```
It's Excel without the formulas getting tangled like Christmas lights.

8.
Let's handle missing data.

```python
CopyEdit
df.isnull().sum()
```
This shows you how many nulls exist per column. Fill them with:

```python
CopyEdit
df.fillna(0)
```
Or drop them entirely:

```python
CopyEdit
df.dropna()
```
Your data is now cleaner, shinier, and ready for analysis.

9.

Want to sort your data?

```python
CopyEdit
df.sort_values("Score", ascending=False)
```
Now your highest scorers are at the top. Sort by multiple columns with a list:

```python
CopyEdit
df.sort_values(["Grade", "Score"])
```
It's like giving your data a priority list. Perfect for reports and dashboards.

10.

Group your data to analyze trends:

```python
CopyEdit
df.groupby("Grade")["Score"].mean()
```
Now you've got average scores by grade. You can also count, sum, or apply custom functions. Grouping is powerful for summarizing huge datasets. Pandas makes pivot tables look like old-school toys.

11.

Writing data back to a file? Easy:

```python
CopyEdit
df.to_csv("clean_data.csv", index=False)
```
This creates a CSV without row numbers. You can also export to Excel:

```python
CopyEdit
df.to_excel("report.xlsx", index=False)
```
Python is now writing spreadsheets for you. Say goodbye to manual data entry forever.

12.
Speaking of Excel, want to **read** from one?

```python
CopyEdit
df = pd.read_excel("grades.xlsx")
```
You'll need the `openpyxl` package for `.xlsx` files:

```bash
CopyEdit
pip install openpyxl
```
You can also specify a sheet:

```python
CopyEdit
pd.read_excel("grades.xlsx", sheet_name="Midterms")
```
Multi-sheet mastery achieved.

13.
Need to combine multiple files? Use `concat()` or `merge()`.

```python
CopyEdit
combined = pd.concat([df1, df2])
```
Or merge by column:

```python
CopyEdit
merged = pd.merge(df1, df2, on="Student ID")
```
Now you're joining datasets like a relational database pro. It's SQL with a pandas twist.

14.
Let's clean some columns.

```python
CopyEdit
df["Name"] = df["Name"].str.strip().str.title()
```
This removes whitespace and capitalizes names properly. String methods in pandas are chainable and powerful. Think of it as spellcheck for your data. You're not just cleaning—you're **polishing**.

15.

Need to rename columns?

```python
CopyEdit
df.rename(columns={"Score": "Final Score"}, inplace=True)
```

This helps when dealing with unclear or inconsistent column names. You can also change the index:

```python
CopyEdit
df.set_index("Student ID", inplace=True)
```

Custom structure = custom control.

16.

Pandas can read and write to tons of formats:

- CSV

- Excel

- JSON

- SQL

- Parquet
  It's like having a universal data translator in your pocket. Just point it to the file—and go.

17.

Want to visualize your data quickly?

```python
CopyEdit
df["Score"].plot(kind="hist")
```

You'll need `matplotlib`:

```bash
CopyEdit
pip install matplotlib
```

Plots are great for spotting trends, outliers, and opportunities to show off. Pandas handles basic charts right out of the box.

18.

Pandas also supports time-series analysis.

```python
CopyEdit
```

```python
df["Date"] = pd.to_datetime(df["Date"])
```
Now you can sort, filter, and group by date or even resample data:

```python
CopyEdit
df.resample("M", on="Date").mean()
```
It's the go-to tool for finance, scheduling, and anyone who thinks in weeks.

19.
Your challenge:

- Read a messy CSV

- Clean whitespace, fill missing values

- Add a column for pass/fail

- Export the cleaned file to Excel
  Boom—you've just done in minutes what used to take hours in Excel. Pandas: your new personal data intern.

20.
Let's recap. Pandas reads, writes, cleans, transforms, and analyzes tabular data. It's powerful, elegant, and surprisingly intuitive once you get the hang of it. With a few lines of code, you can do the work of a spreadsheet army. Combine it with visualization and file I/O, and it's practically a data command center. CSVs bow to it. Excel fears it. You, however, **wield it**.

21.
You're no longer just writing Python—you're writing Python that understands **data**. You can clean it, summarize it, reshape it, and export it like a pro. You've got the eyes of a detective, the hands of a sculptor, and the brain of a spreadsheet whisperer. Pandas puts real-world power at your fingertips. And now you're not just writing scripts—you're writing solutions.

22.
Next up: **The Final Stretch – Packaging and Sharing Your Python Project**. Because what's better than writing awesome code? Sharing it with the world, packaging it right, and maybe—just maybe—becoming a Python rockstar. Let's ship it.

Chapter 22: Power Scripts – Python in the Real World

1.

You've written functions. You've mastered data. You've even tamed the mighty panda. But now it's time to take off the training wheels and roll Python into the **real world**. No more examples. No more `print("Hello, World!")`. You're going to write **power scripts**—bite-sized automation beasts that solve real problems. These aren't school projects. These are scripts that **do things**. Let's ship them.

2.

What is a power script? It's a single Python file that does one thing really well—fast, repeatable, and usually better than a human. It might clean up a folder, rename 200 files, scrape a site, send an email, or monitor a system. It's a **utility knife in code form**. Think "small tool, big impact." You'll find them in sysadmin kits, DevOps pipelines, marketing teams, and even grandma's Windows machine. Because when done right, power scripts are **magic spells you can double-click**.

3.

Let's build one: a folder cleaner.

```python
CopyEdit
import os
import shutil

for filename in os.listdir():
    if filename.endswith(".log"):
        shutil.move(filename, "logs/")
```

Now all your log files are instantly sorted. Wrap it in a function, add `os.makedirs()` with `exist_ok=True`, and boom—you're now tidying the digital house faster than Marie Kondo with caffeine.

4.

Want to make it **interactive**? Add input:

```python
CopyEdit
folder = input("Enter folder name: ")
```

Now it works on any directory. Better yet, use `argparse` to pass arguments via the command line:

```python
CopyEdit
import argparse
parser = argparse.ArgumentParser()
parser.add_argument("folder")
```

```
args = parser.parse_args()
```
Now it's command-line friendly and automation-ready.

5.
Need to run it every day? Schedule it.

- On Windows, use **Task Scheduler**

- On macOS/Linux, use `cron`
  Or create a `.bat` or `.sh` file to trigger the script on boot or at regular intervals. Your script is now a **background worker**. No GUI needed, no hands involved. That's peak automation.

6.
Let's build another one: a **YouTube downloader**.

```bash
CopyEdit
pip install pytube
```
Then:

```python
CopyEdit
from pytube import YouTube
yt = YouTube("https://youtu.be/dQw4w9WgXcQ")
yt.streams.get_highest_resolution().download()
```
Boom—video saved locally. Now you've got a personal digital VHS. Welcome to the offline future.

7.
Want to turn a script into a **desktop app**? Try `tkinter`:

```python
CopyEdit
import tkinter as tk
from tkinter import filedialog
```
Now you can build file pickers, buttons, and input fields in just a few lines. Wrap your script in a GUI, give it to your coworkers, and look like an app developer. Python isn't just backend anymore—it's **front and center**.

8.
Build a PDF merger:

```python
CopyEdit
```

```
from PyPDF2 import PdfMerger
merger = PdfMerger()
merger.append("file1.pdf")
merger.append("file2.pdf")
merger.write("merged.pdf")
merger.close()
```
Congratulations, you just saved someone 30 minutes and three angry Google searches. That's the power of power scripts—**solving real pain** in five lines of bliss.

9.
Turn Python into a clipboard ninja:

python
CopyEdit
```
import pyperclip
text = pyperclip.paste()
pyperclip.copy(text.upper())
```
Now you've built a text transformer. Combine with regex, and you've got a clipboard reformatter for names, dates, or invoice IDs. Keyboard shortcuts meet scripting sorcery.

10.
Make a **website monitor**:

python
CopyEdit
```
import requests

r = requests.get("https://example.com")
if r.status_code != 200:
    print("Website is down!")
```
Add `smtplib` to email alerts. Or `twilio` to text yourself. Suddenly, you've got a tiny, custom monitoring system—tailored and lightning-fast.

11.
Build a **habit tracker**:

python
CopyEdit
```
from datetime import datetime
with open("habits.txt", "a") as f:
    f.write(f"{datetime.now()}: ✅ Python practiced\n")
```
Now every time you run it, it logs your progress. Turn it into a game. Add emojis. Success now fits in a log file.

12.

Don't forget about **data-to-visuals** scripts:

```python
CopyEdit
import matplotlib.pyplot as plt
df.plot(kind="bar")
plt.savefig("chart.png")
```

Grab data, plot it, send it. Weekly reports become auto-pilots. Managers love graphs. And Python **draws better than you**.

13.

Build a script that converts image formats:

```python
CopyEdit
from PIL import Image
img = Image.open("pic.png")
img.save("pic.jpg")
```

Now make it loop through a folder and batch-convert them. Someone will think you're a graphics wizard. Python's secret? It's **quietly brilliant**.

14.

Want to generate random passwords?

```python
CopyEdit
import secrets
import string
alphabet = string.ascii_letters + string.digits +
string.punctuation
password = ''.join(secrets.choice(alphabet) for i in
range(16))
print(password)
```

Add a GUI or save it to a vault. You're now a digital locksmith.

15.

Write a script that **texts you** the weather.

```python
CopyEdit
# Use requests for weather API
# Use Twilio for SMS
```

Now your phone buzzes with custom alerts. Weather, birthdays, stock updates, or cat facts. Python doesn't just run on your computer—it **talks to you**.

16.

Power scripts also play well with **cloud services**. Automate uploads to Dropbox, Google Drive, or AWS S3. Or download backups every week. It's your own DIY sync service. Cheaper than apps. Tailored to your weird workflow.

17.

Create an **image watermarking tool**:

```python
CopyEdit
from PIL import Image, ImageDraw, ImageFont
img = Image.open("photo.jpg")
draw = ImageDraw.Draw(img)
draw.text((10, 10), "© MyBrand", fill="white")
img.save("watermarked.jpg")
```
Boom—branding at scale. Artists, meet your new assistant.

18.

Want to build a script others can run? Use `if __name__ == "__main__":`

```python
CopyEdit
def main():
    # your logic here

if __name__ == "__main__":
    main()
```
This turns your script into a **reusable module** *and* a standalone tool. You're coding responsibly. And professionally.

19.

Distribute your script with:

- GitHub

- PyInstaller (to make .exe files)

- Python packages (via `setuptools`)
  You're not just writing tools—you're **publishing** them. Make your scripts click-to-run and watch the magic spread.

20.

Let's recap. Power scripts solve real problems—fast, automated, and repeatable. They clean folders, manage files, interact with the web, build reports, notify users, and even dance with GUIs. They're small, mighty, and insanely useful. Once you start building them, you'll never stop. Python isn't just a language—it's your new life hack toolbox.

21.

You're now the kind of person who doesn't just accept problems—you automate them out of existence. You've got the tools, the skills, the confidence. You've written scripts that scrape, clean, organize, alert, analyze, and empower. Your laptop is no longer a machine—it's a **digital ally**. The boring stuff? Consider it conquered.

22.

And with that... you've gone from `print("Hello, World!")` to wielding power scripts like a terminal warrior. The next step? Keep building. Keep solving. Keep unleashing Python on your problems, your projects, and your passions. Because with Python in your pocket, the world is **yours to automate**.

Conclusion – Scripts Written, Powers Unleashed

So here we are—you and Python, sitting at the edge of a beautifully automated sunset. Together, you've built functions, tamed pandas, looped your way to freedom, and written scripts that would make your past self weep with joy (or possibly confusion). From slinging text across the screen to downloading data, poking APIs, and even building desktop tools, you've gone full Pythonista. But don't get too comfortable—because Python isn't just a language. It's a *lifestyle*. And this book? It's just your onboarding ritual.

You now hold the power to automate boring things, dominate spreadsheets, hunt down bugs with a vengeance, and even impress that one coworker who still brags about their Excel macros from 2007. And that's saying something. But the real question is… what next? Because once you've harnessed Python, it's hard not to look around and go, "Hey, I wonder what ELSE I can automate, conquer, or completely bend to my will."

Well, I've got good news. Python may have been the start of your journey, but it doesn't have to be the end. In fact, the tech jungle is vast, wild, and oddly acronym-heavy. And I've hacked my way through quite a bit of it—armed with coffee, terminal commands, and a deep love for making the complex... uncomfortably simple. So if you're ready to take your skills beyond the snake, here's a list of other adventures I've written to level you up like a caffeinated sysadmin on a mission:

Other Book Subjects by Scott Markham:

- Active Directory

- AS/400

- Azure

- Barracuda Firewalls

- Big IP F5

- Cisco IDS/IPS

- CompTIA Network+

- Juniper IDS/IPS

- Kubernetes

- Linux

- Microsoft 365 Admin Portal

- MySQL

- OKTA

- Oracle

- Palo Alto Firewalls

- PowerShell

- SCCM

- SQL

- TCP/IP

- Unix

- VMWare

- Wireshark

Whether you want to dive into *Active Directory* and own the domain (pun intended), analyze network traffic like a digital detective with *Wireshark*, or rise from the IT ashes like a phoenix via *Azure*, there's a book waiting for you. You don't have to stop with scripting—you can secure networks, build cloud empires, interrogate packets, manage databases, and boss around entire fleets of endpoints without breaking a sweat (or a production environment).

Maybe Python helped you conquer your first tech mountain, but the rest of these subjects are your trailheads to even greater heights. Whether you're chasing certifications, boosting your resume, starting a side hustle, or just want to be the "cool IT person" at the next staff meeting (trust me, it's a thing), these books are ready to be your guide, your weapon, and possibly your new best friend.

So close this book with confidence, not because the journey is over—but because your skills are just beginning to take root. Let Python continue to be your personal automation sidekick, and let the rest of the IT universe become your playground. And if you ever need help navigating it? Well... you know where to find me.

Until then, keep scripting smart, breaking less, and automating like a caffeinated wizard.

– Scott Markham

.

www.ingramcontent.com/pod-product-compliance
Lightning Source LLC
LaVergne TN
LVHW081530050326
832903LV00025B/1714